signs of love

BY LEONARD FOLEY, O.F.M.

Nihil Obstat:
    Rev. Hilarion Kistner, O.F.M.
    Rev. John J. Jennings

Imprimi Potest:
    Rev. Andrew Fox, O.F.M.
    Provincial

Imprimatur:
    +Daniel E. Pilarczyk, V.G.
    Archdiocese of Cincinnati
    October 12, 1976

The *Nihil Obstat* and *Imprimatur* are a declaration that a book or pamphlet is considered to be free from doctrinal or moral error. It is not implied that those who have granted the *Nihil Obstat* and *Imprimatur* agree with the contents, opinions, or statements expressed.

Cover design by Lawrence Zink

Photographs and illustrations by Michael Reynolds

SBN 0-912228-32-6

Contents

Introduction

"**S**ee how these Christians love one another!" Thus did the pagans of ancient Rome express their amazement at the charity of the early Church. They were seeing what Christ had prayed for to the Father: "that they may be one, as we are one." For many it had the result he prayed for: "so that because of this unity the world may believe that you sent me."

The Church—that is, all the people of the Church—is a sign. It is for human eyes to see, human ears to hear. We believe in the invisible, but we need some assurance that it is there. Indeed, to love is to trust; and faith lives in darkness. But it cannot live without something to cling to—the memory of words actually heard, of a face actually touched, a person actually seen. Where there is no sign of life, there is no life. Where there is no sign of love, there is no love.

Since God made man to live by seeing and hearing and touching, he adapted himself to us, as it were, when he wanted the most perfect union of friendship with us. The Word was made *flesh*. God came to us in a form we could understand in our way, seeing him, hearing him, touching him. His love was made *visible. Christ is the Sacrament of God—the visible sign of God's love.*

The purpose of this book is to consider the extension of this visible life of Christ to the end of time through the visible sacraments of the Church—in fact, through the visible Sacrament which is the Church herself. For the Church as a body is also a visible sign that the Spirit of love is carrying on the redeeming work of Christ.

Christ, in the glory of his resurrection, has entered into a totally new kind of life. This life "shines on the face of the Church," as Vatican II states it. The Church is a sign—a Sacrament—lifted up among the nations.

Vatican II, especially in the Constitution on the Liturgy, has given new prominence to a consideration of the sacraments that stresses the primary importance of the two "fundamental sacraments"—Christ and his Church. The following quotations will set the stage for the discussion that is to follow.

1. Christ the Sacrament Acts in the Sacraments

"By his power Christ is present in the sacraments, so that when a man baptizes it is really Christ who baptizes" (Constitution on the Liturgy, 7).

"The liturgy is an exercise of the priestly office of Jesus Christ. . . . Every liturgical celebration is an action of Christ the priest and of his Body, the

Church" (Constitution on the Liturgy, 7).

2. The Church as Sacrament of Christ

"Christ sent his life-giving Spirit upon his disciples and through his Spirit has established his body, the Church, as the universal Sacrament of salvation" (Constitution on the Church, 48).

"By her relationship to Christ, the Church is a kind of sacrament or sign of intimate union with God, and of the unity of all mankind" (Constitution on the Church, 1).

"From the side of Christ as he slept the sleep of death upon the cross there came forth the wonderful Sacrament that is the whole Church" (Constitution on the Liturgy, 5).

3. The Seven Sacraments as the Visible Signs of Christ Acting in His Church

"The visible signs used by the liturgy to signify invisible divine things have been chosen by Christ or the Church" (Constitution on the Liturgy, 33).

"In the liturgy the sanctification of man is manifested by signs perceptible to the senses" (Constitution on the Liturgy, 7).

4. The Purpose

"The purpose of the sacraments is to sanctify men, to build up the body of Christ, and to give worship of the divine majesty. . . . The sacred liturgy contains abundant instructions for the faithful" (Constitution on the Liturgy, 33).

"This is what we proclaim to you:
what was from the beginning,
what we have *heard,*
what we have *seen* with our eyes,
what we have *looked* upon
and our hands have *touched—*
we speak of the word of life.

This life became visible:
we have seen and bear witness to it,
and we proclaim to you the eternal life
that was present to the Father
and became visible to us."
(The First Letter of St. John, 1:1-2.)

The author gratefully acknowledges a debt of gratitude to the staff of ST. ANTHONY MESSENGER, especially to the editor, Father Jeremy Harrington, to assistant editor Karen Hurley, and to Mary Schroeder of St. Francis Bookshop, Cincinnati, for their encouragement and their enlightening and penetrating comments.

Chapter I

"And This Will Be a Sign to You"

the best signs are person-signs. A dog whimpers when he wants in or out, an apple turns red when it is ripe. But only people can make signs that say, "I trust you," or "I'm sorry I hurt you," or "I will love you all my life."

Signs are the only way people's hearts and minds can contact other people's hearts and minds. Angels don't need signs; there's no need of signs between Father and Son and Spirit.

But when you get to people who are made out of warm flesh filled with spirit, or spirit "em-body-ing" itself in flesh, the only way one human spirit can reach another is through that same "em-*body*-ment." We "reach" each other through our visible bodies.

Eyes speak to eyes. Words speak to ears. A muscular handclasp or a tender caress is a sign one body-person uses to communicate with another. The sweetness of an apple pie or the scent of perfume can be signs of concern and affection between persons.

Human life is filled with sign-making: conversations, arguments, boos, greetings, whispers, children's shouting, quarterbacks' signalling, widows' sobbing. Cold glances, rapturous gazing, open-eyed inquiry. A wink, a sneer, a lifted eyebrow. A letter, an SOS printed in the snow, a "For Sale" sign on the lawn. Standing at attention, slouching in a chair. The shrugging of shoulders, a blow in the face, a supporting hand, waving arms, folded hands. Stink-bombs, incense, a cigar to celebrate the baby's birth. Wine for friends, a spoonful of soup for a sick man.

We human persons just couldn't live without signs. Imagine trying to tell somebody you're thirsty if you couldn't make sight-signs like tipping an imaginary glass to your lips, or sound-signs like "I'm thirsty." Think of the problems of never seeing the expression on others' faces, of never being able to read a letter, or not noticing the flashing light of the police cruiser behind you!

Signs, then, are the ways persons relate to other persons. They are the way our feelings and thoughts and wishes get *outside* us and into other people's feelings and thoughts. They are the way we "come through."

Now if all this seems a long way from a discussion of the sacraments, it may be due to the fact that the sacraments are a long way from being understood as the Father and his Son intend them. God is literally "making signs" to us.

When God wishes to enter into a personal relationship with his sons and daughters, he comes to them *as they are*. After all, he made them body-

persons; it was an idea he had eternally, so we conclude that this seeing-hearing-feeling-touching-smelling-tasting body-person must be a precious part of creation indeed.

Obviously, if God wants man *as man* to see him, he must become literally visible to man's eye. If man is to touch God, and if God is to touch man, God must have some kind of body. And this is precisely what God does in the sacraments. He makes his presence known to our eyes and ears, our taste and sense of touch. We eat bread, we feel the waters of Baptism, we hear the words of confession, we are touched with the oil of anointing. God thus adapted himself to our kind of life by using signs we can understand as human beings. These are the sacraments—the signs of God's love acting, the seven great ways we are assured of his presence.

But there is a most fundamental fact that we must consider before we can understand these "signs of God." We must first consider the greatest sign of God: the FIRST SACRAMENT—*Christ himself*. He is the first and the greatest sign of God.

It is only because Christ became man, and made God visible, that he can now remain visible in the seven sacraments.

Then, having considered the first sacrament, Christ, we will consider the SECOND GREAT SACRAMENT—the Church, the Sacrament of Christ.

Just as there are two "great" commandments of love that underlie the Ten Commandments, so these two "great" sacraments, Christ and the Church, underlie the seven.

Questions For Discussion

1. How are "signs" that human beings give each other different from signs that animals give each other?

2. Why is "signing" an essential part of human nature?

3. What are some effective nonverbal signs we give each other?

4. Are there certain human signs that are understood by people of all races and nations?

5. A wedding ring, the peace greeting at Mass are symbols. How are they different from *mere* signs like "Exit"?

6. Do you believe the statement that all life is sacramental?

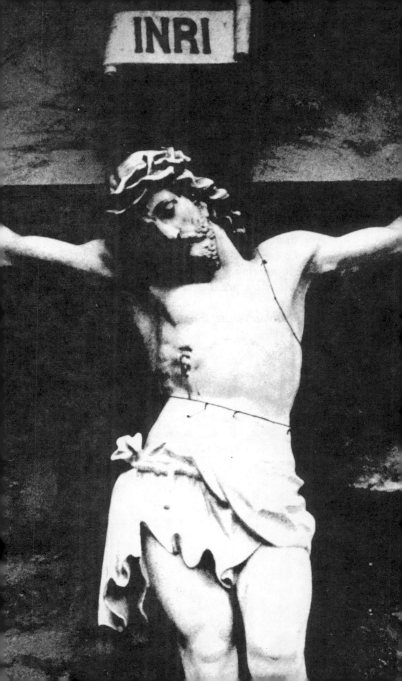

Chapter II

Christ the Sacrament

Jesus, a Sign
from the Father

a leper came up to Jesus and bowed low in front of him. "Sir," he said,"if you will to do so, you can cure me." Jesus stretched out his hand and touched him and said, "I do will it! Be cured! Immediately the man's leprosy disappeared" (Matthew 8:2).

This cure that Jesus brought about is a sacrament, a visible sign of God's loving action. It is a dramatic, person-to-person encounter. Jesus' eyes and words and touch are signs of the Father's love and concern and power. God enters a sick man's person through signs that the receiver can easily read.

This is what happens in every sacrament: just as Jesus brought the Father's healing love to the leper in visible human flesh, so Christ comes to us in visible signs of bread and wine, water, oil, words. In a sense, these are now his "flesh." The basic reality of the sacraments is that a Person comes to us and says, "Certainly I want to! Be cured!" Christ comes to us *visibly* in these signs. It is really himself—not an empty sign. Just as our bodies are living signs of our presence, so his body—and the sacramental signs—are visible assurance of his presence and that of the Father and the Spirit.

As we shall see, it makes no difference that we live centuries after those persons on the pages of the Gospels. We are the sick in mind or body, the dead in heart or flesh, the poor, the lost, the desperate, the weak, the hungry. And the Father is giving us essentially the same Sign he gave them. The same Person comes to us today. St. John tells us that the Eternal Word, the Second Person of the Trinity, "was made flesh and dwelt among us." The humanity of Jesus is the Sign that makes this Word visible. In him we see the Father. Through him we are filled with the Spirit.

It is all-important to emphasize that phrase, *Jesus came to them.* We do not take the initiative with God, though often we think we do. St. John says, "Love, then, consists in this: not that we have loved God but that he has loved us" (I John 4:10). God must love us *first* before we can love him. We do not spring into human or divine life unaided; we do not go about doing good on our own strength, creating something of our own to present for God's approval. This is the heresy that has always hovered near the human heart, and if we are to purify our sacramental disposition, we must begin with one of the basic facts of life: "Without me you can do nothing."

The basic fact of life is that God loves us. He gives us life, embraces us with his love and healing power. He even makes us free in receiving his love.

We can use or not use this freedom, but we cannot use it unless he continues at every second to keep it in existence.

So the first fact of all life is that God is always coming to us. There is not one incident in the Gospels which is not preceded, immediately or remotely, by the phrase, "The Word was made flesh."

Jesus' love is now, as it was then, a love for individuals: his good friends, Mary and Martha and Lazarus, the Twelve, the adulteress, the widow of Naim, the Pharisee who came at night. It was an individual love and it was a love that clearly showed the Father's love. It is the same for us as it was for the people of that day. The Personal Sacrament of God can be intimately present to each of us, because any individual person can meet Christ sacramentally.

The Word-made-visible, Jesus walked among his brothers and sisters. He found them marked with the signs of sin. The Hebrew mind—incapable of thinking of body, mind, soul as "separate parts" of man—saw a dead body as a sign of the universal catastrophe that man's sin had brought upon his world. Sightless eyes, withered legs, useless tongues and ears were the marks of the Evil One.

We are happily moving away from a mistaken notion that our "soul" was the great thing to be "saved," while our body was a sort of hindrance that some day would be removed. "Flesh" had a connotation of unwholesomeness.

But Jesus came as body-spirit to cure whole persons—bodies and spirits inseparably united in

9

life. Jesus, the Sign of Life, erased the dead signs of the sin of man. He touched the body of the widow's son and his touch was a life-giving sign. He simply spoke to a Roman official, and a child was cured. He looked at the paralytic and cured his body and spirit.

That's the key phrase: body *and* spirit. Body-spirit. Not two sometimes-parallel, sometimes-contradictory powers chained together, but a oneness, spirit needing body and body needing spirit. Jesus saw these signs as fulfilling his messianic vocation. When the disciples of John the Baptist came, asking if Jesus was "the one to come," he said, "Go tell John what you have seen and heard: the blind see, the lame walk, lepers are cleansed, the deaf hear, the dead are raised to life" (Luke 7, 22).

Jesus cured bodies because body-healing is part of man's total redemption, as well as a powerful sign of the invisible spirit-healing. He used words and touch, bread and wine to reach man's spirit, because man's spirit can be reached only through its body-counterpart.

The Word was made *flesh*. A Person—the Second of the Trinity—actually took a real human nature—a body-spirit—as his own. There was one Person still—but a divine Person who could now act as man, in a mysterious unity that included not only flesh and spirit, but also human nature and divinity. God did not "turn into" flesh; but human flesh and spirit became as much an instrument of the divine Person of the Word as our bodies are instruments of our spirit.

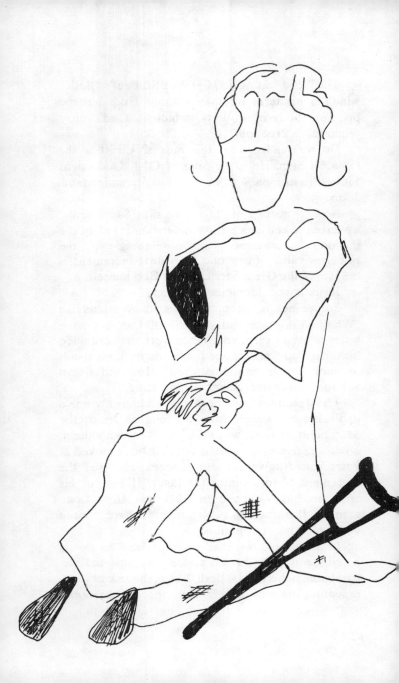

The Word was made *flesh.* Not St. Paul's "flesh," which is his term for man without God, but the priceless body-spirit unity, which is God's most remarkable creation.

Do we realize what this means? Christ is the Greatest Sign. He is the Sign of God. God opens himself to us by a Sign we could easily understand: Jesus.

Now, if instead of "Sign" we say "Sacrament," we have the key idea for the understanding of all the individual sacraments. Far outweighing even the priceless value of any one individual sacrament is the fact of the Great Sacrament of God himself.

Jesus is the Sacrament of God.

Sometimes, in speculation, we ask questions like "When were the apostles baptized? Did they have water poured over them? When were they ordained bishops? Did Christ place his hands on their heads or anoint their hands with oil? How did Christ administer the sacrament of anointing?"

The questions have been made childishly naive to illustrate a simple fact: As long as Jesus, the Sacrament of God, was visibly present with them, *no other sacraments were needed.* If Jesus looked at Peter with forgiveness and concern, *that* was the sacrament of forgiveness for Peter. If he put his arms around the children, *that* was Holy Communion. If he said to twelve men, "I have chosen you," *that* was ordination.

In a moment, we shall consider how all this is possible now that Christ is no longer visible-audible-touchable in his mortal flesh. But at the risk of over-repeating, let us say again: the *Fundamental*

Sacrament is Christ, then and now. He is the em-
body-ment, the Sign of God's love.

Today the Risen Christ, whose human nature—
flesh and spirit—has been perfectly glorified by the
Father, reigns as Lord and King of heaven and
earth. In this supremely happy Christ there remains
the love of the Father which carried him through a
life of perfect and visible pouring forth of his
Father's love for his sons and daughters on earth.

This is the Christ we meet in the sacramental
signs today. Now *with us* he visibly offers to his
Father the joyful and generous love of a son—a
human, em-body-ed Son.

Because there was a Jesus truly human who
could say with the greatest enthusiasm—facing the
prospect of misunderstanding, rejection and death,
"Of course I want to cure you!" we can be certain
through faith that the glorious Christ, the victorious
risen one, speaks the same words to us today, in his
sacramental actions.

One of the most forceful statements of this fact
was made by Pope Leo the Great: "Whatever was
visible in our Redeemer has passed over into the
sacraments." What Christ's activity in his mortal
body *was* when that body was visible *is* now his
sacramental activity in his sacramental community,
the visible Church of faith and love. The Church is
now the sign of Christ's continuing presence among
men. The individual sacraments are visible en-
counters wherein we can be just as certain as were
the people long ago when Jesus touched their ailing
bodies, that the Father is acting in our lives, that his
Spirit fills our very being.

The resurrection and ascension, therefore, do not involve a separation of Christ and his followers, but a new, all-pervading, though invisible, presence.

As Vatican II emphasizes: "By his power he is present in the sacraments, so that when a man baptizes it is Christ who baptizes." If we apply this principle completely, we must realize that it is the living Christ, God and man, who stands in the midst of his brothers and sisters at Mass. It is the personal Christ who heals and raises to life in confession; it is Christ who here and now sends his Spirit in Confirmation. It is Christ who consecrates a priest and establishes man and woman as signs of his creative love in marriage. It is Christ who comes to the bedside of the sick.

To this Christ each of us—and all of us together—are visibly joined when we celebrate his sacramental actions today. The meaning of his life, death and resurrection is that all of us, in our enspirited-bodies and embodied-spirits, can enter into that attitude that was visible and audible and touchable in his earthly life and on the cross, and which is still present in his heart today. The sacramental acts of Christ in the Church are the visible signs that he is continuing to draw us into his own attitude and spirit of love for the Father, an attitude that is received and given by human signs.

We cannot think of the sacraments as *things,* therefore, just as we cannot think of a mother holding a baby, a friend clasping the hand of a friend, a husband and wife embracing, a nurse carefully helping an old man to walk—as people merely doing *things.*

What a tragedy if that's all they were!

Going to confession is not doing some*thing.* Mass is not something that is an obligation. The prayer of Anointing is not a magical formula. The sacraments are not lifeless containers of a lifeless something called "grace."

A sacrament is the way God goes "outward." An outward sign. The Great Sign of God acting visibly today. He comes visibly to join our whole person to himself who is Eternal Spirit, Grace, Love.

An outward sign of inward grace. But not a "thing" instituted by Christ. Rather, Christ himself, Sign in a new way, a new mode.

If we say, in faith, "If you will to do so, you can cure me," we will hear and see, in visible signs, the absolute assurance of divine love: "I do will it! Be alive. Be cured. Live in me."

Questions For Discussion

1. Would you say that Jesus is the "sacrament" of God? His body? His visible presence on earth? His invisible presence?
2. In what sense are people signs of God?
3. Did people need other sacraments when Jesus was visibly present with them?
4. What were Jesus' healings a "sign" of?
5. Compare Jesus and the seven sacraments as signs.

Chapter III

The Church as Sacrament

All of Us Are
One Sacrament

the actual body of Christ is not visible anywhere in the world today as he was in his mortal body. Yet we have just seen that Christ *is* visible in the world today, in the sacraments.

It should be obvious immediately that Christ is not visible in a group of material objects like water, bread, wine, oil *taken by themselves.*

It is only when these things are used by people in a very special way that they truly become the visible signs of Christ.

Christ did not just leave instructions on the use of bread and wine and oil. He gave symbols to *persons* to use in faith, hope and love, and without these the symbols are meaningless.

There are many beautiful "signs" that men and women use to express their inner feelings, convictions and decisions. It is not demeaning of these precious human signs to say that they cannot be the "Christ-signs," unless they have a connection with Christ that is somehow visibly asserted at the time they are used. For instance, an intimate meal shared by a close-knit Jewish family is a beautiful sign of their love for each other. But in fact it is not the Christian sacrifice-meal-sign of union in Christ, because they do not intend it to be that. It is good, but it is not the same good thing we refer to when we speak of Christian sacraments.

The full picture of the sacraments, therefore, must include the faith-community which publicly declares itself to be "sacramentalizing" the acts of Christ today. It is the faith of Catholics that Christ did give an essential structure to his Church, in order that there might be an identifiable public witness to his continuing activity on earth, a group which has all the essentials—visible and invisible— of being Christian.

Catholics hold that this essential "organization" of the Church began with the choosing of twelve men to be the official witnesses of Christ's life, death and resurrection, his appointing Peter to be their leader, and his commission to all of them to proclaim the good news to all nations, to teach with authority what he had given them and to continue his sacramental actions. The successors of these twelve today, Catholics hold, are the Bishop of Rome, the Pope, and the other bishops of the world united with him.

This is not the place to discuss the ecumenical movement. But it should be evident that one of its greatest difficulties concerns the "structure" within which the sacraments are visible. Can there be the Eucharistic meal Christ directed his followers to have if those who take part in it have important disagreements as to its meaning? As to the nature of his presence? As to who is actually commissioned to make it a "Christ-act"? Happily, Christians of good will are sincerely approaching these problems in Christian charity and solid historical scholarship.

Having stated this position of Catholics, however, we must be equally careful not to identify "the Church" with the Pope and bishops, and to think that the sacraments are "things" entirely under the control of the bishops and their helper-priests, passed out like CARE packages to the "rest" of the Church, the lowly laymen.

No Pope, bishop or priest in the world can "give" a sacrament, unless someone wants to receive "it."

The Church is, we must remember, the Body of Christ. The whole Church celebrates the sacraments, not just the priests who confer them. It would be sacrilegious to make a sacramental act of Christ visibly present unless those who are to receive and respond to his love are present and willing to do so.

Here let us simply approach the basic fact of Christianity. Christ wants to give us *God's kind of life eternally.* God's kind of life is love. The Father and Son and Spirit are one God in community, giving and receiving infinite love. Life is love. Christian men and women, then, must have one distinguishable characteristic: to love *with the love of Christ;* to love God, and to express this same love visibly to all men as Christ did.

The Church does not just have unity of structure. That is important, but it is useless and un-Christian if the structure does not serve something infinitely more important: Christian love, visible unity in the spirit of Christ's love. (If all of us, Catholics and Protestants, were more concerned about this love, the problems of structure might become less important.)

What is the Christian Church, then? It is a visible union of those who publicly say to the world: *we show you Christ today.*

The Church is never so much the Church as when Christians gather, as *Christians,* to celebrate the activity of Christ that is visible in the sacramental actions they share.

Christ remains visible today. Why? To fulfill his purpose of drawing all men to his Father in charity for each other.

The point of all this is: the Church — *the whole Church* — is a sacrament too. Christ, we have seen, is the Sacrament of God. The Church is the Sacrament of Christ. If anyone wants to be assured and touched by Christ today, he can come in faith to the visible Christian community in its sacramental faith-actions.

This explains why there has been so much emphasis lately on the communal celebration of the sacraments. The very essence of the Eucharist is that it is a breaking of bread—that is, the sign of unity of the many who eat the one loaf in charity, and drink from the one cup. It is this unity in Christ that was the very reason Christ came. Our purpose is to become perfectly united in spirit with the sacrifice of Christ. His sacrifice was his perfect love of his Father and of his brothers and sisters. The one is inseparable from the other.

(The sacrament of Penance presents a "community" problem. We will discuss this further in a separate chapter. But let us remember, for the moment, that the early Church's primary use of the sacrament was the *visible* reconciliation of public sinners to the visible community of the Church from which they had knowingly cut themselves off.)

Baptism is the birth of a new Christian into the Christian community of Christ. The Christian community celebrates the new "little church" formed within it at marriage; the whole Christian community is interested in the new representatives of Christ who are publicly made so, in the sacrament of Holy Orders; the whole community is concerned as Christ visibly strengthens the seriously sick persons. The whole community welcomes the Christian being made an adult in Confirmation.

The Christian community contains all these elements. But obviously, the whole Christian Church cannot physically gather around one altar. Obviously, no entire diocese, not even all the members of a parish, can always be present for the sacramental acts of the community. But the ideal towards which every sacrament points is the visible unity of all Christians in their love of God and man. Christians are most visibly Christian when they partake in the visible acts of Christ today. And the more they are filled with the spirit of Christ's concern for each other, the more they will want their comings-together to be exactly what Christ prayed they would be—signs of Christ—life-and-love to each other and to the world. Only then are they doing the Father's will.

One can be too idealistic in this, of course. The Church, i.e., the community of Christ, is made up of all kinds of persons: those whose faith has developed to deep commitment; those who are barely able to stay in the community; people of all temperaments, educational and cultural backgrounds, physical, spiritual and emotional conditions. No given group—parish or sub-parish—will ever celebrate the sacramental acts perfectly. The very attempt to express their oneness involves emotional and spiritual acceptance of each other, openness, forgiveness, and at least implicit apology for one's own faults.

Community adjustment is terribly difficult. It is easier to make the sacraments a private affair.

A little boy once knelt at the Communion rail of his parish church before a statue. Not a single "vigil light" was burning. So, with heroic self-denial, he fished from his pocket one of the two dimes that were his entire bank account, slipped the coin into the slot, and lighted a candle. As he went aside to put the burnt match into a waste basket, an elderly lady happened to approach the Communion rail and knelt down right in front of the candle he had lighted. The boy hesitated, then knelt down near her. She prayed fervently, but apparently had no intention of lighting a candle. He squirmed uncomfortably for a moment or two, and then whispered to the startled lady with only an edge of anger in his boyish voice: "Why don't you pray on your own candle?"

We all like privacy, even our own candle. Many older people today were raised in a liturgy that did not emphasize this all-important communitarian aspect of the liturgy. Community was there, but it was sometimes expressed (except at Italian weddings and Polish Baptisms) in a rather restrained, formal way. Sometimes, at least, Sunday Mass might almost have seemed like many people simultaneously making a *private* visit to the Blessed Sacrament.

It will be difficult for many to continue to adapt to what seems to them an unwarranted "togetherness" in the sacraments. Overzealous leaders who are determined to "enforce" community "even if it kills you" are only making a naturally difficult problem more so.

What this chapter has tried to show is that the Church is never so much the Church as when she is visible as such. She is visible in the faith-actions of her members. These are publicly identifiable as such when the members of the Church come together as a body in sacramental activity. Then the body of Christ shows the Spirit of Christ.

The love which is characteristic of Christianity should not be evident only *after* Mass. It should be most evident in the sign which is itself the *expression* of the love of Christ that is already present and a strengthening of this love for the future.

Christ prayed at the first celebration of the community meal-sacrifice: "Father, may they be one, as you are in me and I in you, *so that the world may believe it was you who sent me*." In other words, the oneness of Christians in Christ's love will be the reason the world will come to believe in Christ, and in the Father through him. Now, this love must be *visible*. It is indeed seen in the ordinary Christian's daily life. But the moment when he is most visibly Christian is that time when, in visible community with his brothers and sisters, he celebrates the acts of Christ.

Only within these two great fundamental truths can the individual sacraments be understood: *Christ is the Sacrament of God; the Church is the Sacrament of Christ.*

Those who saw Christ were seeing God. Those who touched him were touching God. Those who listened to him speak, with human words, out of a human mind, were listening to God.

Now that Christ is no longer visible in a mortal body, he remains visible in the faith-actions of those whom he has joined together into one. All those who have been baptized, and are thus publicly sealed and "certified" as his own—these make his saving action visible in the world today. There is no time or place when Christ is so "visible" as when his visible Body, the Christian community, comes together in faith and love to celebrate the Eucharist. He is already present in his members. But in their faith-action around the altar he becomes so visible that he can be taken as food and drink. In this, as in the other sacramental actions, his saving activity is as tangible as it was when he walked the roads of Galilee and Judea.

And we can be just as sure now, as then, that Jesus Christ continues to function as a sign of the Father's love, revealing the will of God.

Questions For Discussion

1. If Christ is the sacrament of God, what is the one great sacrament of Christ?

2. What is the difference between a Jewish family lovingly breaking bread together and a Christian family celebrating the Eucharist?

3. What is the final purpose of the Church as sacrament?

4. What does all this have to say about the conduct of Christians?

5. What is the sacrament of Christ — the whole Church, or the parish, or both?

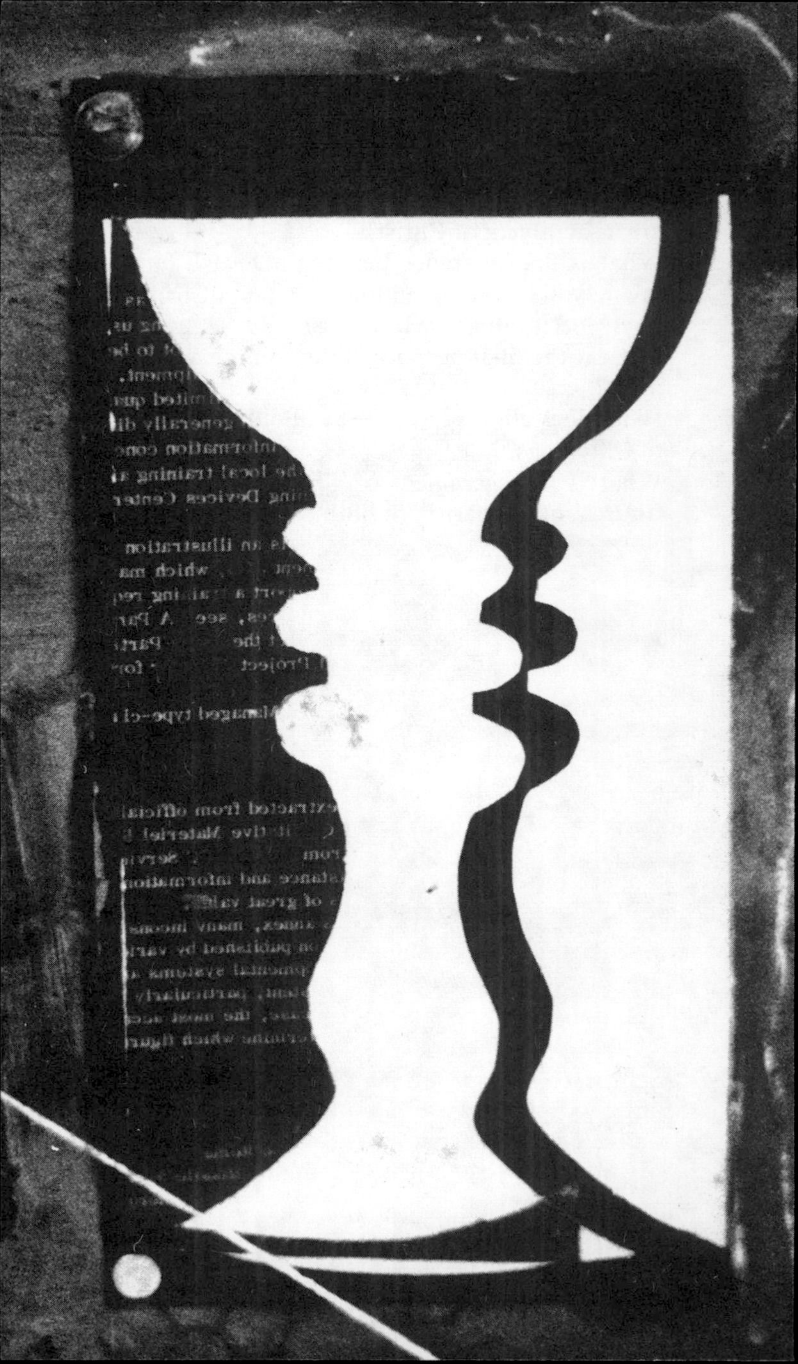

Chapter IV

Attitude

"They Think That by Saying Many Words . . ."

ove, then, consists in this: not that we have loved God but that he has loved us." (I John 4:10). It is all-important to remind ourselves of this basic fact of our life. The sacraments are not magical devices to manipulate God's will; nor are they "holy" acts of our own creation, putting God in our debt. They are meetings with the Christ who comes on his own initiative to save us by reuniting us to the Father.

On the other hand, God does not manipulate *us* either, as if we were puppets. He gives us freedom and wants us to use it. He wants us to respond to his revealing of himself with a corresponding revealing of our own hearts—a full, free, trusting, response of faith. He cannot save us unless we really want to be saved; he will not force us.

The worst thing ever said about Nazareth is recorded by Matthew and Mark. "He did not work many miracles there *because of their lack of faith* " (Matthew 13:58). He *could* work no miracle there— apart from curing a few who were sick by laying hands on them—so much did their *lack of faith* distress him" (Mark 6:5).

On the other hand, we have all been struck by the generosity of Christ to those who came to him in complete childlike trust—or who, like Peter, at last learned to do so. He had only one question for the blind men who prayed, "Have pity on us, Son of David." He said, "Are you confident I can do this?" When they expressed their firm belief, he said, "Because of your faith it shall be done to you" (Matthew 10:27). When the Gentile centurion said those supremely trustful words, "Sir, I am not worthy to have you under my roof. Just give an order and my boy will get better" (Matthew 8:8), Christ told the people that he had not found such faith even among his Jewish brothers and sisters.

Our attitude in approaching Christ in the sacraments is like that of the woman in the Gospels who said: "If only I can touch his cloak, I shall get well." The sacraments are more than the cloak of Christ today, and the power will go forth from Christ as much as we want him to give it. The more spirit we show in trying to see him with the eyes of faith, like the whole-souled Zacchaeus climbing the tree, the more he will be glad to enter our hearts. The more our public meeting with Christ is an expression of love, as it was in the penitent woman who came to kneel at his feet, the more can he say, with the happiness of his vocation as Savior, "Your faith has saved you; go in peace." Perhaps our answer to Christ may even approach some of the full, calm trust of Mary, who expressed her confidence in him in a simple statement, "They have no wine."

Keeping the necessity of this attitude in mind will help us avoid one of the greatest dangers in using ritual: the apparent use of *magic*.

Magic means that a man thinks he can, by his own initiative, manipulate God. By means of a formula that is fully and correctly carried out, he hopes to acquire a certain amount of divine power.

If the witches put the right ingredients in the boiling pot, the right "answer" will appear. If the right colors are used, the exact words are pronounced, the formula is said exactly, the "special" motions of the hands are made at the stroke of midnight, the crops will be good.

Speaking carelessly about the sacraments, we can easily give the impression that they are magic. It may sound like the description of magic, to some people, if we say that certain "things" called sacraments confer grace (also, apparently, a thing) by the very fact that some *thing* is done. We may not help matters by saying that the Church guarantees results if they (again, apparently, things) are "done" right. They seem to be holy things from which we scoop up basketfuls of a commodity called grace, as long as we follow the prescribed routine.

If we constantly emphasize that the sacraments take effect, as the Latin phrase has it, *"ex opere operato"*— that is, from the "work" itself being done, from the action having been performed—it is possible to think that they "work," so to speak, without anything or anyone else being needed.

The expression *ex opere operato* is the guarantee of God's *faithfulness*. It means the Church's actions in Christ can never be emptied of their meaning. Our salvation has been won. Christ is risen, victorious, glorified, Lord of heaven and earth. He has, we can be absolutely certain, sent his Spirit. Human nature is inseparably joined to Christ and made holy in Christ. It is not possible for sin and death and the devil to continue the enslavement of mankind. Christ is not making some kind of effort that could possibly fail; he is not on his way to a *possible* goal. It is finished; it is complete. Now he is joining us to his victory.

God has given his word—his own Word, literally. And the Word has made his Body an infallible sacrament, an unfailing sign, of his saving will. His seven sacraments are permanent and divine assurance of the presence of the saving Christ.

It is true that God has infallibly promised grace to other faith-actions too, like praying in the name of Jesus for his saving grace. But this prayer, though God enlivens it, is fragile. It can weaken and die. The sacraments, being living signs which are the visibility of his risen body today, cannot weaken or lose their force.

So the whole matter of *ex opere operato* is about *God,* not ourselves. It assures us that these are *divine* signs. We must not make them magic signs.

Redemption is not a banking system. Christ does not deposit a certain amount of *something*—grace, capital—and give us the sacraments as blank checks to fill out. Rather we are, *sacramentally,* drawn into a more and more personal life with Christ by meeting him more generously, more openly, each time we celebrate his visible signs, and through him

are joined to the Father and the Spirit, actually communicating in the love of the Trinity.

The matter of our disposition, then, is of primary concern. Going to the opposite extreme from magic, we try to accept in our own person the actual attitude of Jesus, our now-risen Lord. For the purpose of all his sacraments, the purpose of his Church, is that we be joined to, we *possess*, his attitude of perfect love of the Father. Jesus directed men's attention to the Father and told all men they too could be sons of God. The Father "reigns" in us, his kingdom is fulfilled in us, when we receive from Christ the power to be totally possessed by the Father's love as he was.

If we read the signs right, we will be helped by that very fact to fulfill Christ's intention. The very reception of the sacraments in faith and sincerity is a powerful help to disposing us properly. They enkindle—if received with faith—*new* faith; greater hope, if received in hope; more Christlike charity, if approached with a sincere attempt to acquire the generous will of Christ.

These considerations point up the importance of a real preparation for the meeting of Christ in the sacraments, and a proper "thanksgiving."

A wholehearted celebration of the sacraments is both a result and a cause. Our disposition at the moment is important; our disposition long before and long after is important. We are, in a sense, always, preparing for Mass, Communion, confession, Anointing, by the way we think about Christ's presence all the time. It is obvious, moreover, what a great difference it will make in the fruitfulness of the sacramental meeting if we truly "re-collect" our minds for a period before approaching, "fanning the flame that might otherwise lie dormant."

Father Karl Rahner, in a famous chapter in his book, *Christian Commitment,* has emphasized this fact about thanksgiving after Mass. It is just not possible, he says, to say everything we would like to say during the rather quick, formal celebration of the liturgy. The all-important dispositions need to be filled out, as it were, after the actual celebration. The impulses of grace need to be savored, the very meaning of what we have done needs to dawn upon our minds. This immediate thanksgiving will then merge more effectively into a continuing attitude which will, gradually at least, make our whole lives truly Christlike.

Faith and the sacraments are not, therefore, two separate compartments of our life. The sacraments are signs of faith, and their fruitfulness will be proportionate to our faith. They presuppose it, they nourish it. They express it visibly, they deepen it invisibly. They are the signs of the faith of the Church, indeed; but the faith of the Church, again, must not be fossilized into some magic "thing" which works wonders no matter what is present in my own heart. The faith of the Church is that which exists in all the living individuals who make up the body of Christ. So, in the end, without pride, without self-sufficiency, I must say that salvation—mine, and that of others, the saving of the world by the sacramental work of Christ today—does indeed depend on me. Christ can save only individuals.

He does indeed save us as *members.* We are

nothing if not social beings. But I can be a responsible member only if I am a responsible *individual*, standing on my own two feet and accepting God's gift.

Perhaps we can best express this by reminding ourselves of a twofold element in Christ's love. He *comes to* us, bringing the Father's love; he *goes "back" with* us in worship of the Father.

If we think of all Christ did as *saving worship,* we will be aware of the elements that must be present in our own attitude: welcoming Christ's saving us, and worshiping the Father with him.

Saving worship, then, not magic. Not a lifeless group of Christians going through motions that somehow "count" as fulfilling their obligation. But the divinely-assured sign that Christ is filling the world with his healing presence, and that he is taking man to the Father in loving worship.

If our many sacramental meetings seem to have little effect, perhaps we should ask ourselves if we are like his own home town of Nazareth: incapable of receiving miracles because of lack of faith. It is not that we disbelieve the saving presence of the Risen Lord; but it is terribly easy to fall into the rut of mere externalism, formalism and the suspicion of magic. White magic, but still magic.

Let us summarize: just as Jesus is the Sacrament of God, so the Church—the visible community of those who bear his name—is the Sacrament of Jesus. The whole Church is Sacrament. Within the Church we have the individual sacramental actions.

And in a further carrying out of this meaning of "sacrament" we, as individuals, have a further dignity. Having met Christ the Sacrament in the actions of the Church, we each go forth to be "personal sacraments" of Jesus to the world. Our lives are signs of what he is doing! Our charity, both as individuals and as members of a community, is to be the reason the world will believe.

Thus we have a divinely given way of showing the light of Christ to the world. As the Council said, the light of Christ must shine on the face of his Church.

We are that face. The world is watching it for signs of life.

Questions For Discussion

1. What does it mean to say that the sacraments work *ex opere operato*? What does it *not* mean?
2. How would you describe a "magical" view of the sacraments? What is the origin of such a view? How would you counteract it?
3. What does it mean to be saved by Jesus? When does this happen?
4. Apart from what God does, what is the most important human factor in the sacraments?

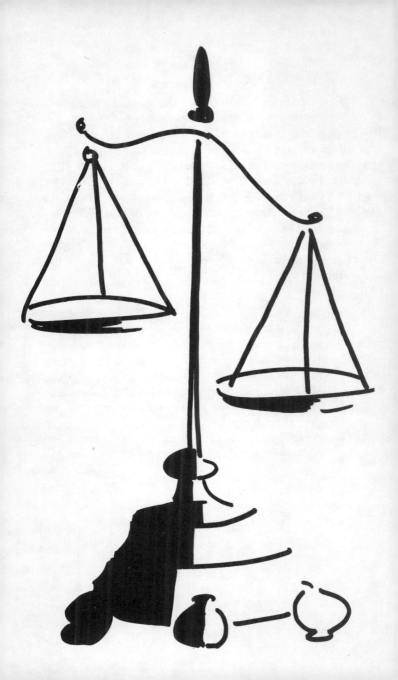

Chapter V

Grace

Wrong Question:
"How Much Do I Get?"

mathematics deals in problems. But sometimes mathematics *itself* is the problem, when we try to use a mathematical mentality in dealing with spiritual realities. Love is not a matter of inches or ounces.

It would be easier to ignore the "mathematics" of the sacraments and begin ticking off the sacraments one by one. But somebody will raise the question sooner or later, so we might as well wrestle with it now.

The mathematical problem arises from the fact that we can measure *how many times* we do something, and *how much quantity* of time, money, energy is involved in what we do. If doing something once is good, is twice better? If visiting the sick for an hour is good, is a two-hour visit better? We are not angels. We deal in sizes—10, 42, a dollar's worth, three acres, two pints. If *some is* good, *is more* better?

If I love you and give you a cheeseburger, would I love you twice as much if I gave you two cheeseburgers?

The problem arises from the fact that, on the one hand, we can make judgments only according to what is visible to our senses (at least until they perfect mental telepathy), and secondly, there is never enough visible to make an *adequate* judgment about things that have no quantity—love, grace, guilt.

But it is only human to try to *measure* goodness. Who loves you the most? How can you tell? Our Lord said, "By their fruits you shall know them." I can know that this is a good man, because he is faithful (a matter of time, partly), patient, forgiving, self-controlled while at the same time showing courage and frankness when these are called for. When there are two men like this, who has "more" holiness? I don't know.

The mathematical problem arises from the fact that we live from day to day, and find ourselves repeating all kinds of things: eating, breathing, saying hello, kissing, mowing the lawn, sending birthday cards, taking showers, singing *The Star-Spangled Banner* and saluting lieutenants.

Why keep on doing things? Is there value in numbers?

The problem is concretely expressed in that supposedly devastating remark made by an exasperated husband whose wife complained that he never told her that he loved her: "I married you, didn't I?"

She was saying she needed a continuing visible expression of love. He was saying, "So what's mathematics got to do with it?"

There are many good people who have absorbed, along with deep faith and real Christian love, a rather mathematical way of talking about the sacraments. The reason they go to confession, they say, is to "get more graces."

What they mean is true, of course: they are drawn more intimately into the relationship of love with the Father in Christ. Their lives are enriched, their faith-commitment to God is deepened. God's love possesses their persons more fully.

But the words sound as if these individuals were building up piles of shining gold bars in heaven, gradually filling their particular vault with mathematically increasing guarantees of happiness on deposit in the heavenly bank. On that great "Come-and-Get-It Day" there will be the great inheriting.

There is no wish to ridicule, by this comparison, anyone who uses the expression "to get more grace." But the purpose of this book is to help all of us increase our appreciation of the real Christ-presence, the personal-ness, of the sacramental acts; the unmeasurable love; the personal, not mathematical, relationship; the continuing attitude that alone gives value to external acts; the impossibility of measuring grace.

It is foolhardy to try to cover the subject of grace in a few pages, though catechisms do it all the time. But let us try.

"Grace" means "gratis." Free, for nothing. Not deserved, not paid for, not earned. A "gracious" person simply gives, another receives. And so we say "Gracias, amigo!" I am saying "grace" for your graciousness.

Gratis is *how* something is given, not *what*. Unfortunately, we have so stressed the fact that God's grace is absolutely gratuitous that we sometimes forget *what* is so gratuitously given: a personal relationship.

When you ask children what grace is, they usually answer that it is a "gift." Absolutely true! But so is sunshine, digestion, and those ties Dad gets for Christmas.

"What" is "it"?

"It" is not an "it." The gift God gives with supreme "gratisness" is himself. He communicates his own intimate life. His life is love, eternal giving and receiving in the communion of the Father, the Son and the Spirit.

Obviously he cannot make me his equal. The Father cannot make me God. But he can so fill my person with his presence, his living, his loving, his power, that I can act like him! I can have a personal relationship with him "on his level," as it were. I can do things only God can do, i.e., I can love like God, I can be loved like God, I can "see" God because he has lifted me to his level. It's like the statue Pygmalion becoming the living girl who can now fall in love with the sculptor.

So, God offers man, through the visible sacrament of Christ, an intimate personal relationship of life and love. God's kingdom, his "reign," is his possessing the persons of free men. They welcome God's "taking them over" completely. His will becomes their will, his attitude their attitude, his love their love.

So, viewed from God's side, *grace is God's love*

enfolding us all and speaking to each one of us. Viewed from man's side, grace means a mysterious new life in our whole being.

Grace is God's entering into communion with man, freely, gratuitously. It is personal communion with God. He did not give man just *any* kind of relationship; he gave him one that involves sharing his own life, or, as St. Peter said, a sharing of his own nature. God did not make statues, even statues that turned into people, like Pygmalion; he created children who live his life, not (what might have been but never was) merely human life without any reference to himself.

The important point to remember is that God is not communicating *something*. He is communicating *himself*. HE is grace.

Well, what happens to the man or woman with whom God thus enters into communion? Isn't there *something in* them?

There are no comparisons, but let's try one anyway. Mother and father give a child life. Does he have something? Yes, life. What does the child of God have? God's life. The child is not more alive when he's sixteen than when he's six. His life is not measured by how tall he is. His human life is measured by the *quality* of the way he is a person— his free and wise attitudes and actions. So God's grace in us is not something measurable; it is a *quality*. It is *life*, not measurable in quantity, but capable of being enriched, deepened, made "more" like the spirit of the unmeasurable God.

What do we mean, then, by "habitual" or "sanctifying" grace? Is it *something*?

It is God permanently offering and communicating himself to man and even giving him the power to accept the relationship freely in faith, hope and love. It is man permanently receiving the power to live in that relationship, on a level of life that can simply be called divine, because the power that "runs" it, the reasons why it acts, and the love with which it acts comes from this personal self-communication of God.

What is "actual" grace, then? Here we have an unfortunate choice of word. "Actual" wasn't chosen to make sure we realize that grace is "real"; it is, of course, but that isn't the point here. What "actual" was originally meant to express was the fact that all our *"acts"* in God's life are his gift too. In other words, God shares all the acts of our life. His life consecrates all the particulars of our existence. It is personal communion in personal life as it is lived in concrete circumstances.

When this gracious love of God meets man in various situations, birth, reconciliation, worship, marriage, etc., we speak of *"sacramental"* graces, but again, we must not think of these as so many individual "things." In Penance we meet Christ as forgiver; in Eucharist as the one who nourishes us, unites us, worships; in Baptism as the one who gives a new birth to a totally new life.

Throughout, there is a *quality* in us, a reality, a life, which we call grace. It has no parts, it cannot be measured, IT is not an IT.

To say that one "goes to" a sacrament means that one meets God acting visibly in Christ's sacramental actions. There is no more of mathematics involved than in the meeting of two friends.

It is a mystery, as all love and life is a mystery. We must not pin it, like a butterfly, on a botanist's board. Butterflies must fly.

Questions For Discussion

1. Can one "get" a greater quantity of grace? If so, how? If not, what can one get "more" of?
2. If grace is not an "it," what is "it"?
3. If you had to teach an adult about grace, what comparisons would you use? If you had to teach a child?
4. Do you think every situation in life is a means of grace?
5. Do you know a better word than "actual" for "actual grace"?

Chapter VI

Gradual Growth

Wrong Question: "How Long Does It Last?"

s Baptism all over at the last Amen, when the baby is taken home and the priest closes the baptismal font? Is the sacrament of confession "finished" when the penitent walks out of the confessional?

When the bride and groom dash from church to the wedding breakfast, when newly ordained priests file from the sanctuary, "Is that all there is"?

If we say that *visibility* is one of the essentials of sacrament, then it would seem that the sacraments are "over" when their visibility is gone.

Let us see where this would lead us. It would be rather silly, wouldn't it, to think that Christ gathers his community visibly together to celebrate a wedding and then has no more to do with the couple! It is absurd to think that all Christ had in mind was that a man and woman stand up in church and state that they are now becoming living images of the love that exists between Christ and his Church, and that this *statement* is enough. The public act and statement, the visibility, as we have seen, is essential; it makes a sacrament what it is. But it does not restrict the activity of Christ. His personal presence, active friendship and blessing, so vividly assured in the sacrament, surely are not turned off like a faucet after the ceremony.

How long does it continue? Let's stay with marriage. Since marriage is for the lifetime of the two, Christ must be publicly saying that he will *show* himself in all the activities of this husband and wife and fill them with his own quality of life and love. (Whether they allow him to do that is not the question here.)

The one gracious God who surrounds our whole life with his grace, i.e., his freely given love, is giving public and absolute assurance that he will be present to this married couple, *as married,* for life.

Similarly, Holy Orders will "last" for the life of the priest. Anointing of the sick means the special activity of Christ for this sick person *as sick*, obviously as long as the sickness lasts.

Asking the same questions about Baptism, we have to say that this visible act has *eternal* results. That is, by this one resurrection, a person is born to divine life and will live forever in that life. (Again, whether he accepts God's love is not the question here. Baptism is forever.)

Just as one can never become "not born" after he has left his mother's womb, so it is impossible for anyone who was baptized in faith to become "not born" to God in eternal life. He has a life he can enjoy forever or ruin forever. But he can never again be what he was before he was re-born in Baptism.

Now we come to two sacraments that present a problem in this matter of repetition. And since the question concerns them both in more or less the same way, we will consider only the "repetition" of the Eucharist and leave a discussion of the frequency of confession until later.

The Eucharist

Let us ask a silly question, only for the purpose of understanding the depth of meaning in the Eucharistic sacrifice. Why isn't Eucharist done once and for all, like Baptism, Confirmation, Holy Orders and marriage? Even the reconciliation of the mortal sinner is presumably once and for all. And Anointing is for the whole duration of a sickness. God's love, visibly shown, does not "wear out." So why should there not be a Eucharist once and for all? Why do we have Eucharist weekly, even daily?

The first answer might be that such a once-and-for-all action has been done in Baptism. We are born to eternal life, we accept Christ totally, we are consecrated as members of his body. There is nothing more basic that can be done to relate us to God and to the Church.

There isn't?

That's like saying that once you're born there's really nothing left to do. Birth is "final." We are totally persons; nothing needs to be added.

Nothing?

A newborn baby is indeed a person. There is a certain fullness which makes a baby infinitely precious already. He now has the rights of a person.

But he is mostly the *promise* of personhood to be developed. He needs many other persons to

47

become "somebody." (Even as adults, we are indeed persons, yet who would deny that he or she is still *becoming* a person?) But right now the baby needs his father and mother and countless other people all through his life to *love him into being* a full person. A baby will die or be seriously damaged for life, not only if he is not given food for his mouth, but also if he is not given visible, feelable, hearable, tastable, smellable love for his person. And he will need this every day of his life. No "once-and-for-all" here!

He grows to full life by what can be called half of life: the ongoing *receiving* of others' love. Dozens of people coo over him, keep him warm, feed him, guard him, gradually make him realize he is worthwhile. He is *somebody*. All the care and concern gradually convinces him that he is worth loving. People are *continually* fulfilling his needs, giving him what is necessary for growth in body and emotion and spirit.

Gradually, he begins to realize (how long does it take us?) that the other half of life is *giving*. If he gradually grows out of the natural selfishness of babyhood (how long does it take us?), he senses that, if life grows by receiving, somebody must be doing the giving!

As he passes through the phases of childhood and adolescence, someone may try to express very clearly the fundamental fact of life: this giving-and-receiving is at the heart of all relationships—family, friends, strangers—and with God himself.

And that's life! The happiness of giving and receiving. And that is one of the essentials of the Eucharist: the Christian community.

Man Cuts the Lifeline

It would be beautiful if everything worked out the way God wants it to work out. But we know it doesn't. It's not all that rosy. First of all, we know that we ourselves have often forgotten that we must *receive* God into our lives; secondly, as a natural result, we have forgotten that we must *give* to our neighbor. In other words, all of us decide in many subtle ways that we really don't need God, and that we don't need our neighbor either, still less that we "need" to give him anything. (After all, we say charity begins at home, doesn't it?)

So the world always has a tendency to fall apart, to collapse into billions of selfish little pieces; man alienated from God, man alienated from man.

Man cannot "put it together" again. He cannot save himself alone. We need a mediator, a middleman, someone who saves us by bringing the Father to us, and by taking us to the Father.

Into this alienated world Jesus came, to save us. He reasserted the truth that all goodness is from the Father, and the Good News is that the Father wants to give us all goodness. He gave his life in simple generosity and service to the Father, and to his brothers and sisters.

He gave his life and received it back, gloriously, unbelievably. And he will spend the rest of time getting men to believe the giving-receiving secret of the eternal God.

He left a giving-receiving community for the world to watch, so that it would be evident exactly what he meant. The Church, that is, the whole community of Christians visibly united, is the "body" of Christ. The comparison cannot be pressed too far, but the main point is evident: if each of us is alive with the life of God, possessing our persons by the action of the Spirit of Christ, then what we do in that same Spirit is *his* doing. And since we are a *visible* community, we can be called the "body" of Christ. The Church is the "body" of people who say to the world that they have received everything, even eternal life, in Christ; they show the world the giving-receiving love of Christ himself.

The greatest visible coming-together of this Body is in Eucharistic celebration. For Christ has given us one great commandment: love one another as I have loved you. He gave us one sign above all to perform: come together, he said, and show that my Spirit really is making you one in love with each other, with me, and with the Father. Show this by the everyday sign of unity in a family—the family meal. Break one loaf and give the pieces to everybody present, as a sign that you are actually one in spirit, giving and receiving each other's love. Eat my flesh and drink my blood together, to show what's already present and to make it better for the future.

So the Eucharist brings together the deepest elements of life: giving and receiving; the source of all life and happiness; and the actual means of avoiding the fatal selfishness of not giving, not receiving.

Maturity for little Johnny, we saw, was his gradually beginning to realize that love is a two-way street.

Gradual. That's the key word. Who is mature? Who ever gives and receives perfectly? Whose motives are entirely free from at least a wisp of selfishness? Who is ready to give what he can, as it is needed? Who is ready to be open to the love of his brothers and sisters, knowing that even in receiving their love he is recognizing more of their needs? None of us.

And so we keep coming back to this action wherein the eternal secret of life, and God's plans for our life, are *visible,* the *Eucharist.*

Unlike all other sacraments (though marriage comes close) this is the sacrament for all life, the sign that expresses our whole life and God's whole plan.

We are nowhere near fulfilling it, but we are on the way.

Evidently then (it has taken a long time to get here, I admit) the very nature of Eucharist is that it is part of the growth of our life. It is like the other things that we repeat in our life—nourishment, talking to other people, wanting to meet friends again and again.

Husband and wife don't just meet each other once a year. Friends don't have dinner once and say, "Well, that's it, for life. It was nice knowing you." Life is continuing, growing, maturing.

For the same reason Christians must develop a continuing practice of expressing visibly the deepest dimension of their lives. They keep on coming together in Eucharist. Though they are painfully aware that they do not always love each other as they should, they come back again and again to the altar, express their sorrow, and celebrate the miracle that love has already worked in their lives, and receive once more the strength of Christ himself to try again.

There are probably many aspects of our celebration of Mass that are unsatisfying to some Catholics. But the Mass is much better than it looks. It is a visible sign that Christ has succeeded this much in healing the basic tragedy of the world, man's refusal to love. It is a promise that peace is possible.

Questions For Discussion

1. In what ways does the comparison of birth and growth illustrate the once-and-for-all and yet continuing nature of the sacraments?
2. How long does the grace of a sacrament "last"?
3. What two things must happen to a baby so that he or she can become a whole person?
4. What is the most common sin of mankind?
5. Why isn't it enough to express your love once and for all?

Chapter VII

The Heart of the Matter: One in Christ

espite all our troubles today, we've gotten rid of a lot of pain and messiness. At least we have covered it over. Garbage is pretty well packaged, at least in the suburbs. Death is given the most expert cosmetic treatment. Ultimately, we feel, all diseases will be healed. We have the softest of garments, chairs, beds. We speed about in air-conditioned cars, sit in cool theaters, eat food to which the magic of man has added to the taste nature gave. We can learn what is going on any place in the world by wire and wireless, and by the magic screen with the colored dots racing across it. We can watch people getting killed without even the inconvenience of doing anything about it, because we're not really there. Even sin has been attractively packaged, so it can be viewed in antiseptic detachment and satisfaction—whether it be loveless sex, or "legal" brutality, or "political" lying, or "disciplinary" injustice. True, we will all die some day, but it's a great show while it lasts, eh? They give you morphine on the last days, anyway. Then it's all over.

What are we being saved from? We don't need any savior! Saved *for* what? Let's have it all right here!

Brave new world! Can a Christian "argue" with it, that it really ought to be running scared? That a man can mess up his life forever? How can you tell someone he's not having a good time?

A Christian is one who admits that he's not as happy as he wants to be. He believes in a God who wants to give him more happiness than he can imagine. He believes that mankind at large is sick, in body and spirit, and doomed to die, and that within the sickness and death there is already healing and life, a life being transformed into an eternal happiness beyond belief. He believes that only God is good, and that wherever there is goodness, there is God; wherever there is unhappiness, God has been deliberately excluded.

But he believes most in a Father who keeps running down the road to embrace his prodigal children in all their rags, because he has begotten them. They are the fruit of his love, they came from him, and he wants to be with them forever.

Most of all, Christians believe in a God who came to serve them, who gets down on his knees and washes their feet, to teach them how to be saved from their despair, and their fear of loving each other.

The Christian believes that there's a hell to be saved from, and a home to be saved for. He believes that both heaven and hell are starting now, on earth.

He believes in a Spirit that gently pours the

healing of Christ into the bodies and souls of the brothers and sisters of Christ, quietly leading them, bashful and suspicious, toward a center. And as they near the center, they aren't as afraid of each other as they were on the dark fringes of life. As they reach the center they are face to face with the Eternal God, and they recognize that the center was in them all the while. It was there from the beginning.

The central fact of Christianity is that God is more eager to heal us than we are to be healed; that he is more interested in our happiness than we are; that he makes us free even if we use that freedom to crucify his Son; that he uses the worst thing we could devise—the death of his Son—as the way of raising us up from the worst thing that can happen to us—eternal death of body and soul.

Jesus accepted our kind of life: mortal, limited, inheriting pain and death. Without sin, he suffered the "lowest" point of our existence—death. He was raised up from the depths of our misery, and we are raised with him.

He saved us by coming to be one of us, so that by being with him we would be safe. He was one flesh with us. He went through the transformation we needed. Because we are with him, we can go through the same transformation he did. Life is our Passover, and the Eucharist is the visible celebration of it.

Passover: We Are Saved

The Old Testament presents difficulties to the modern reader. But it has one simple and clear message: There is one God, and he is good. The core of Jewish faith was that God loved his people faithfully. He was tender to them, "as one who touches the cheek of an infant."

The Old Testament isn't for history buffs. It is for the people of St. Mel's in Middleville, Illinois, next Sunday, at the 10 o'clock Mass. What happened in Exodus is happening in Middleville.

If you're going to heal all the people in a city of two million, you have to start *some* place. You pick three, four, ten doctors, nurses, to be a nucleus of the healing that you hope will extend to all citizens.

God picked the Jews to be his nucleus. He put a Moses at their head and got them out of the ghettos of Egypt. He made them a people, free, religious, united. He made a pact with them: he would be their God, and they would be his people.

The great covenant on Mt. Sinai was celebrated by a sacrifice and a meal. Moses took the blood of an animal and poured it on a stone altar; the altar stood for God. He threw the rest of the blood on the people. (They had vivid liturgy in those days!) It meant that in them and God there was one life, one union: Father and children, King and people, Husband and bride. They ate together: God's part in the meal was symbolically shown by burning the fat of the animal: the fragrant aroma was symbolically "spiritual" for the Spirit of God to enjoy.

Now the important thing is that down through the centuries, every year, the Jews celebrated Passover. The feast was a kind of "making present" of the Passover-saving by God long before. Their prayers each year even said as much: "It was not with our fathers (only) that you made the covenant:

it is with *us*" (Deut. 5:3).

They always saw God as the one who was saving them, had saved them, would save them. They were saved by belonging to his chosen people. Sometimes they betrayed him, and he punished them. Even when the Temple was destroyed—indeed, almost the nation itself—in two exiles, they still looked forward to the saving God. He would send a Restorer.

Gradually they talked of a New Exodus; there was promise of a New Covenant, a new saving.

And so there came the day when the lambs were being slaughtered for the Passover sacrifice. In an upper room, Jesus said, "I greatly desired to eat *this* Passover with you before I suffer" (Luke 22:15).

Now Jesus would be the fulfillment of the original Passover. The last perfect step in man's transformation to God's own life would take place.

Jesus shared all the ills of mankind except the perversion of freedom we call sin. He would save man from the worst that was happening to him: death, slavery of the devil, sin, suffering, sickness, unhappiness; and he would save him *for* what God had planned in the first place: eternal happiness in the face-to-face communion with the eternal God.

So the Passover was the transformation of man to God's life. The transformation would take place in this man, and thus with human nature. Because he would then, even as man, be lifted up to the height of glory, anyone who is *with him* can have the same transformation to eternal glory.

But first Jesus had to "pass over" himself. He went to the lowest possible level of our misery:

death. He had already embraced human nature in all its limitations, suffering, weakness. Now he would plunge into the darkness.

The Gospels say Jesus was terrified at the prospect of death. He literally sweat his own blood in fear as he faced the darkness of the grave. But he would identify himself completely with his brothers and sisters.

Thus, in terrible agony, his body being crushed with pain, his feelings raw with fear, his mind and imagination threatened with the terror of dying, *he made the supreme act of love of his Father.* He said "Thy will be done." This was not a "giving in" to some sort of stubborness of his Father demanding that he suffer a certain amount of pain, which would presumably "satisfy" the Father. It was the faithful, trusting gift of himself, carried out in the most unselfish spirit and in the most demanding of circumstances.

What was perfect about Christ? The fact that he was willing to show the creature's absolute dependence on God. He gave himself simply, absolutely; his death said that all life belongs to God, that man must trust God absolutely.

There is nothing greater a man can give than his life. So Christ was willing to give up life, with all the terror that attends death, as a sign that he was a real man: God's true child, one who trusted absolutely. He was saying: the only way your·children can be healed and made alive and eternally happy, my Father, is if they let you lift them up. They must not think they are God. They can do nothing. They can only receive. You want to give them everything, but

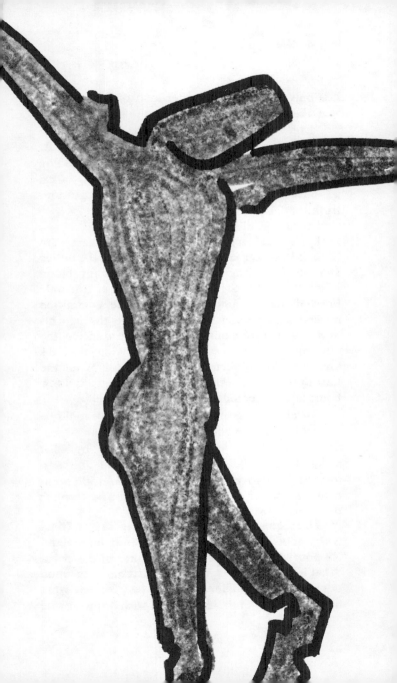

it is only if they receive *your* kind of life and love that they will be happy.

"I place myself entirely in your hands. I commend my spirit to you. I freely lay down my life. At the heart of my terror is a calm 'I trust you.' You alone are master, not a master who lords it over us; a God who alone is God: I submit to this glorious truth, and I am. . .

LIFTED UP!"

Easter, Calvary, the Last Supper. All three are Christ's Passover and ours. First he made the public and ritual offering of himself. "This is my blood which IS BEING SHED for you." He thus solemnly fulfilled the meaning of Passover. He committed himself with perfect willingness to go through his own Passover from death to glory. The sacrifice, the offering of willingness and the receiving of God's love, was already perfect *within* his heart. When the final onslaught of terror came in Gethsemani a few hours later, he could say "Thy will be done!"

For all time he said the New Passover should be a meal of brothers and sisters. For the transformation of man can be accomplished only by what makes God to be God: love. Man will be transformed if the love of God flows *into him*, then *out from him* to his brothers and sisters, and through them back to the Father.

The second great element we celebrate in Mass is the actual carrying out of Christ's commitment. He poured his own blood on the altar of the cross. What irony there was in the cry "His blood be upon us and upon our children." That was precisely what he was doing. The New Moses was throwing the blood that meant union of life with God out upon that crowd, and then out beyond its edges, until it flowed upon the last sorry fringes of mankind.

Now the "sacramental-ness" of Christ was complete. He was the sign of God's love come visible to man. Now he visibly and actually gave the final concrete sign of love. He carried out the sacrifice of the Last Supper by actually giving the breath of his body to God. He leaped trusting into the terrible darkness.

He had done all he could do, as Man.

Then the third act of the Passover. "God lifted him up, and gave him glory."

We have no doubts that Christ was God. Let us not forget that he was man. He was a real man, he lived and died and offered himself as a real man. And his humanity was transformed, lifted up out of the death he willingly suffered. His humanity was raised to supreme glory; this is the final and deepest meaning of our salvation. We are saved from all that is evil; we are saved for eternal glory. What happened to Jesus is happening and will happen to us.

How does it happen? How are we transformed in Christ? How do we enter into Christ's Passover?

The *act and the attitude* of Christ in his Passover is made present to us so that we may share it—the act and the attitude. He is not merely present as, for instance, a book on our desk is "present." By the visible sacraments he is present with the attitude of perfect love for the Father which filled everything he did, especially his death. His dying and rising—his transformation from mortal life to risen life—is made present to us so that we may share this transformation now by the life of God that already possesses us.

When we go to Mass on Sunday, we are trying to receive more and more of this life of God transforming us through the re-presenting of Christ's Passover.

Like the Jews celebrating Passover, we are saying, "It was not only our fathers that Jesus joined to his passing over; we too have passed over with him."

We are now being transformed. We have been born into God's New People, we have God's life. But the new wine is still in the old bottles. We have a long way to go. Like children, we need to be nursed into strength, kept alive, kept healthy, healed of weakness and of the sin we somehow manage to continue.

So again and again we come back to the altar stone where the blood of God is poured out, and we have that blood literally thrown out into the assembled people. We again nourish our Christian persons with the manna in the desert. Christ literally multiplies the loaves again. Again and again Christ kneels down to his brothers and sisters and says: Show the world *this* kind of love. Be my sacrament. Let my light shine on your faces. Show the world who I am.

So, Sunday after Sunday, the people of God, sometimes strangely like the refugee Israelites who straggled out of Egypt, whined in the desert, adored strange gods, come back to the one table to be drawn visibly once more into the very attitude and action of Christ, to absorb more deeply his Spirit.

Every Sunday the Father of the Prodigal Son says, "Let us celebrate. You are my sons and daughters who were dead, and now you are alive. Let me fill you again with my Spirit. Let us sit down again as friends, and I will nourish you again with the very life of my Son."

Questions For Discussion

1. What kind of God do Christians believe in?
2. How did Jesus save us? What does he save us from?
3. What was the Jews' greatest yearly celebration? Why? Do we still celebrate the same thing?
4. Discuss the three ways Jesus was "lifted up."
5. What should happen to us at Eucharist on Sundays?

Chapter VIII

Eucharist

Wrong Question:
"Do I Have To Go?"

Catholics "have" to go to Mass on Sunday. Many of them feel this obligation is the only distinguishing mark of Catholicism that remains. Fish on Friday is gone, you can't tell the sisters without a program, confessions have dropped to a minimum, and the kids are wearing peace symbols instead of scapular medals.

From what a number of parents are saying, there must be a widespread problem of getting the teen-agers to go to Sunday Mass. Apparently a significant number of college boys and girls, at least temporarily, have dropped out altogether.

Among the many who do go to Mass on Sunday, there seems to be a majority who more or less represent the human condition which is partly happy and partly unhappy with the "changes."

But a number—who can tell how many?—resent being told to SING! and hate shaking hands with total strangers, or even with their spouses. They wonder why they just can't be left alone to pray to God in peace.

Others feel the whole thing is just "dead." The Mass doesn't *mean* anything. The hymns are dirges, the readings are unintelligible, the response is apathetic, the atmosphere is heavy with obligation-fulfilling.

We've got trouble right here in River City.

There is no one answer, of course, that will satisfy every objection. But if we can bypass our emotional anguish, there is one consideration that simply outweighs all others: Christ is present and visibly acting in his present-day body, his community. Can anything compare with this fact?

It is possible, of course, to imagine a situation in which circumstances drown out the value. Ten rock groups playing full blast all during Mass would do it. A priest facing the wall and saying everything in Latin might do it for some. A totally hypocritical racist congregation singing pious hymns would make it impossible for a Christian to participate.

But are circumstances ever *that* bad? If Francis of Assisi could show reverence to priests who gave him the Body of Christ even though they might persecute him, we may well forgive the limitations of our own parish priest. If Christ ate with publicans and sinners in his day, we had better be careful about thinking ourselves too good for "hypocritical" congregations today.

The truth is, of course, that we live in a sinful world. Christ has made the saving of the whole world a possibility. But he can redeem any individual person only insofar as—and when—that person actually accepts his healing love.

So the Church on earth is redeemed, but it is

also *being* redeemed, which is another way of saying that it is more or less sinful.

So the Church will always be imperfect. Every Christian meeting will have its limitations and defects, as it always has (look up the "hypocrisy" of Ananias and Sapphira, and the story of the factions in Corinth).

In fact, when you get right down to it, the very purpose of going to Mass is that "our redemption *is exercised*" (Constitution on the Liturgy, 2). We are on our way. Some are hobbling, some are still partially blind, traces of Babel division are still in our words. There are still factions, still ignorance, still selfishness.

But still Christ is in us.

We are sinful people and we never achieve our ideals. But our ideals remain. We are all hypocritical to a degree. But if we wait until there are no sinners, there will never be another Mass— and there would be no need for one. So, in spite of the danger of sounding idealistic and even "ethereal," as one man put it, we have no choice but to say something like the following in answer to the question, "Why go to Mass?" This is the ideal toward which we are painfully striving:

"We go to Mass literally to be the visible Body of Christ coming together in oneness and charity. We do this to be part of the saving worship of Christ, our Head. He is saving us by gradually healing our selfishness and replacing it with his kind of love of his Father and his brother. Saving us, he at the same time worships his Father perfectly, in us, with us, for us.

We go to Mass to express what love we already have for each other, poor as it might be; we go to Mass to deepen our love of God and man.

We go to Mass as a group of sinful people. We publicly confess to the world and to each other that the light of Christ has shone poorly on our collective and individual face.

It all sounds very good. Why doesn't it "look" that way on Sunday? Because we are an imperfect, limping lot of pilgrims. The road is long, there are lots of alluring sideshows, our bodies are sick and our souls are tired; even our friends sometimes hurt us, and most people don't even bother to hurt us.

Maybe there's something to be saved *from* after all!

What's the heart of it all, then? It's a man who is God, and our faith in him. For us Christians he is the beginning and end of our lives. He is everything. Without him, there is nothing, but darkness and eternal despair.

Lord, I believe. Help my unbelief.

But the young will still say:"That's fine, but I can love Christ on my own. In the Peace Corps, in true love and friendship, in quiet places, in silence, in laughter."

But the Christian body must sometimes act as a body. Sometimes they will come together to be, in their meal, the sign of the presence of Christ in his world, reaching out to all men.

A body that's all "pieces" is not a body. A body is united. The Body of Christ must be one, also, not just "spiritually" one, but visibly, bodily one, because love must bring people together or it is not really love at all.

So we sometimes struggle to Mass, because the Mass is our greatest way of expressing the deepest meaning of our life. Life is being willing to go out of myself to others—flesh-and-blood others, who sometimes are (like myself) emotionally damaged, spiritually fatigued, intellectually confused, and sometimes suffering from B. O.

This is where Life heals life. God visibly touches the bodies of his children with his own flesh. He sends the torrent of his own eternal life into them.

And life does go on, and up—painfully, joyfully, incompletely, certainly, doubtfully.

But Life is here, and he will be ours forever.

We celebrate life, then. Half-dead, we open our mouths and creation begins all over again.

Next Sunday. Some joy, some pain. But Life is there.

Wouldn't it be hell if there weren't any Life?

Questions For Discussion

1. If there were no Church law requiring attendance at Mass on Sunday, what reasons would you still have for going?
2. Could Church authority simply leave it up to individuals whether they ever go to Mass or not?
3. When do you think there will be a perfect community celebrating the Eucharist on Sunday?
4. What conclusions do you draw from the third question about what our attitude and expectations should be in going to Mass on Sunday?
5. What is the only hope we have for a "good" Eucharist, for salvation, for hope, for life?

Chapter IX

Eucharist

Sacrifice: Giving or Receiving?

One of the unintended blasphemies in our thinking about God is the strange notion that he's a cosmic Shylock, forever demanding his pound of flesh. Christians are supposed to forgive one another, but does God ever take revenge?

First cousin to this heresy is the idea that pain pleases God. Got a headache? Good! You have something to offer to God. Cancer developing? Great! It can make you a saint!

Continuing this gruesome illogic, we could think that the greatest event in salvation was the *pain* in the body and soul of a man nailed to a tree, spread-eagled and naked: that when the pain finally reached its unbelievable threshold in this man, the Father was finally satisfied, and now everybody can go to heaven!

Let's start over.

God's very being is life. God's very being is love. God freely chooses to create persons with a capacity for eternal happiness with him; he offers a person-to-person relationship with all human persons.

He really wants to be *with them*. He really wants them to be *with him*. He comes to them in their own flesh, to serve them.

To be one with God is to be holy. Holiness is God's very life, his being, his love. There is no holiness but God's holiness. He gives it to his children. If God comes to us, we are holy. If we leave God, we become evil.

The word "sacrifice" comes from two Latin words which mean "to make holy" or "to do something holy." If only God is holy, and only God can make *us* holy, then only God can really "offer" sacrifice. He offers us his holiness. He permits us to enter into a relationship with him in a holy action in which we "do something holy."

It is comforting to know that all through history man has attempted to respond to the realization that God was offering him something. Whatever the distorted forms this took, there was at least an attempt to be on good terms with God, or god, or the gods.

But we are Christians. We believe that the sacrifice of Christ is the center of human history. Our attempt to understand sacrifice, then, should start with him.

Christ is God and Christ is man. True God and true man. He is, therefore: 1) God *offering* something to us. Christ is the Sacrament of God's love. *God* does something in sacrifice; 2) He is Man *receiving* and *responding* to God's offer.

The greatest giving and the greatest responding are therefore centered in this mysterious being who is both God and man, Christ. He *is* sacrifice. He is the only one who makes holy, he is the one made most perfectly holy.

What happened in Christ? He is the Sacrament of God's coming to us in love; he is the visible Sacrament of all mankind's receiving and responding. He is the perfect fullfillment of the oneness of God and man—the heart of the eternal plan of God.

If we really take Jesus' manhood seriously, then we believe that *as man* he was offered holiness, perfect human union with the Father. *As man* he did indeed perfectly open himself to the offer of his Father. He simply opened himself one hundred percent to all his Father wanted to give him. He loved, trusted, hoped, obeyed, *responded* as man. Whatever he did was infinitely valuable because he was God; it was the greatest human good because he was the greatest human being.

But as he joined mankind to his receiving and responding, he destroyed the obstacles: sin, death, evil, the devil, sickness, suffering.

The obstacle to sacrifice, to the possibility of man's being made holy, was sin and the results of sin. How would Christ destroy it?

He not only responded perfectly as man to the love of his Father; he responded as one of the banished children of Eve, as one subject to all the weakness and limitations of sinful mankind, even death. He became as much a "typical" man as he could; he accepted everything but sin. Paul has a daring way of saying it: "God made the sinless one into *sin* that we might become the goodness of God."

He went to the lowest level of man's fall—*death*, trusting his Father would raise him up. He identified himself with man at his most fallen and damaged condition (obviously except for sin) and because his Father wanted to raise man up to the heights he intended eternally.

So Jesus himself went through a transformation that is to be our transformation. He who was holy was treated as if he were not holy, as if he were guilty of sin and therefore deserved death.

He plunged, in fear and agony, but in trust, into the darkness of earth. He trusted his father.

Now the Father's plan could be carried out: he could be one with *a man*, and thereby with all men, because that man, Jesus, had opened himself completely to his Father's offer of love. *A man,* who would begin history all over again as the New Adam, had done what the first Adam had refused to do: he let God possess him completely. He simply put himself totally into the hands of his Father.

Why death? Because that was man's "lowest" point, indeed. He submitted to death because it was the greatest act of trust in God a man could perform. Nothing could better show man's complete willingness to be open to God's will and God's love, to trust him absolutely, than to be willing to submit even to execution and to trust that his Father would bring about a transformation from that most insane of human events.

"With man, this is impossible. With God, all things are possible." Or, as St. Paul keeps saying: "It is all God's doing."

Sacrifice, therefore, is primarily God's initiative.

It is God offering oneness, holiness, friendship, happiness.

But man is not a stone water jar, made to receive something without responding. Only God can give him freedom, but God *has* given him freedom. Man's very personhood, his maturing to life and happiness, consists in using the gift of intelligence and freedom God is offering—and receiving and responding to God's offer of grace, his very life.

Man must indeed *do* something. He must open himself to God's giving, as Jesus did. Even the power to do this is a gift of God, but the gift has been given. It is like the power of a bud to open to the sun.

The Attitude of Christ

What does it mean to offer the sacrifice of the Mass, then? Among countless other things, it means *continuing to be made holy* by accepting more and more deeply the attitude of Christ and therefore the love of God.

At the heart of the sacrifice was the heart of a man. The way to God is through the heart of Christ, literally opened by a man-made spear. At the center of life is a relationship: father to son, father to daughter, brother to sister, brother to brother. Making all this possible is the one who is the perfect human Son of the Father, and the perfect Brother to all of us.

Everything gets down to this, then: that I develop the attitude of Jesus—the willingness, the love, the trust, the openness, the courage, the absolute dependence on the Father.

If the Mass could be put into one paragraph—it

can't—that paragraph might be: "Dear Father! We are your children, with your Son. We thank you for your Spirit, your love, uniting us as sons and daughters, brothers and sisters. You have made us alive with your life; you have opened us to the generosity of your love; you have given us your own life of community."

Questions For Discussion

1. What is ordinarily meant by a "sacrifice"? What do we mean when we speak of the sacrifice of the Mass?
2. Can you think of Jesus as truly human also, and therefore responding to the Father's making him holy?
3. What can we do to imitate the response of Jesus?
4. What is the only thing we have to offer to God?

Six Acts of Christ in His Eucharistic Community

The following sacraments flow from the nature of the eucharistic community which is the Sacrament of Christ, the Church. Through these actions of the Church Christ makes his own action visible in six dramatic and decisive situations in the life of his individual member. The following order seems best for the purpose of study.

Two sacraments for the structure of the community:

MARRIAGE: Christ forms his "little churches."

PRIESTHOOD: Christ appears in visible centers of unity.

Two of the sacraments of initiation:

BAPTISM: Christ makes persons living members of himself by rebirth.

CONFIRMATION: Christ gives his Spirit for mature visible witness in the world.

(EUCHARIST, the *third* sacrament of initiation, has already been discussed in preceding chapters.)

Two sacraments of healing:

ANOINTING: Christ turns sickness from a liability into an asset.

PENANCE: Christ brings reconciliation when his members are unfaithful.

Chapter X

Marriage

Without All the "Little Churches," There Wouldn't Be . . .

If the Church is the sacrament of Christ, marriage is the sacrament of the Church. Family life is the Church in miniature. Psychology is "in." It's so far "in," in fact, that it's probably already on its way "out." Before it is restored to the safekeeping of professionals, however, there are one or two things that all of us, amateur Jungs and professional Freuds, ought to copy down and paste on the bathroom mirror. One of them is:

If you want to become yourself, go out of yourself to other persons; and you must help others do the same. This is another way of saying that no man is an island. Recognition of the same truth is involved in the most devilish torture man has devised for his fellow man: solitary confinement. And it was revealed to us in word and deed: "Whoever would save his life will lose it, but whoever loses his life for my sake will find it" (Matthew 16:25.)

The heart of life is *relationship:* love, friendship,

society, marriage, family. We become ourselves by being with other persons. And at the center of all life is the special relationship which is the first one described in Scripture: "It is not good for man to be alone. I shall make him a helpmate."

Obviously this is the cornerstone of the society God intended to build. It was through the mutual person-creating love of man and woman that God wanted the world to grow into his image and likeness. Man, wife, child: what they are to each other is what they *are*.

But while it is not good for man to be alone, man and wife being together doesn't always work well either. They are not always "good" for each other. At least not good enough, in attaining that independence and freedom of spirit whereby they can give themselves totally to God and each other. They fail by depending on *something* rather than on giving and receiving unselfishly from God and from each other.

God goes out of himself to give man his life. When man rejects this life, there can be only one result: death. Man and woman—mankind—lose themselves in trying to "save" themselves independently. They kill something they cannot re-create.

But even as they sin, God surrounds them with his healing. When the time is ripe, he walks back into their lives as one of their children. Jesus comes to them to show that human life will work, that love is possible.

As has been said so often in this book, Christ is the Sacrament of God. He makes God's love visible, touchable, en-fleshed, human-spirited. He is the sign of the absolute perfection of God's love for man.

Christ is literally the "marriage' of God and man. The comparison was used in the Old Testament, when God "espoused" the virgin, Israel, winning her to himself in the desert. And in the New Testament St. Paul speaks of the marriage of Christians as a revelation of the love of Christ and his Church.

The Church, as the body which Christ joined to himself, is the sacrament or sign of his healing presence in the world. The unity and love of the members are his light shining in the darkness of fallen humanity.

But, in order to have the "big" Church, there must be a multitude of "little churches,"—sacramental life-signs of the presence and love of Christ in the world. The total love of man and wife, the body-spirit union of marriage, is the sign of the body-spirit union between God and man in Christ, and the sign of the body-spirit union between Christ and his members.

What About the Unmarried?

The question invariably arises: what about all the other members of Christ—the young, the widows and widowers, the single, the religious?

What is "special" about husbands and wives that one of the seven great signs of Christ's visible acting today should be devoted to them? Are they, in some sense, more fully Christian than the unmarried because of this special sacramental aspect of their lives?

Let's go back, for a moment. The full initiation of a Christian is accomplished by the three sacramental acts of Christ giving birth (Baptism) and the power of mature witness (Confirmation) and uniting Christians in the sacrifice-meal of unity and love (Eucharist). There is nothing "greater" that can happen to anyone, Pope, priest, nun, husband or wife, than to be thus fully en-membered into the redemptive and worshipping acts of Christ in the world today.

But there is an essential need of life, and a particular dedication for that need, which can be achieved only in marriage: the bringing of new life into the world, and the particular covenant of love which is necessary if this new life is to be nurtured to personal maturity.

If, as the psychologists (and common sense) have discovered, we are able to "go out of" ourselves and become persons only if we are assured that somebody loves us "out there," then obviously there must be a great ability to love on the part of those who bring children into the world. Their "creative" love is the visible sign of God's creative love for all his children. It is therefore a sign of God's visible creative love in Christ. Parents "create" persons by loving them into being, from conception to maturity.

God made marriage a unique expression of human love: it is total, body and spirit; it is lifelong; and it is destined for fruitfulness. No other love-relationship in life has these distinctive qualities, though of course other relationships have distinctive sign-values of their own.

And so this **already sacred** relationship of man and woman in marriage was, inevitably, we might say, a perfect sign for the new relationship between God and man won for us by the visible Christ, the love of God made flesh.

The love of Christian men and women in marriage is a sign of the totality of God's love for us *in Christ;* it is a sign of the faithfulness as well as the fruitfulness of God's love for us *in Christ.*

There is at least one professor of dogmatic theology who begins his lectures on the sacraments with marriage, not with Baptism or Eucharist. He does so for this reason: if Christ is the Sacrament of God, and the Church is the Sacrament of Christ, then the greatest sacrament of "church" and unity of persons is husband and wife. If Christ came to redeem all life, and to insist on the good of all creation, where can this statement be better made than in the circle of the family?

The importance of the Incarnation is not just that Christ became man but that he became man *in our circumstances,* in the concrete situation of human life, as it is. If there was any natural symbol or sign that Christ might use to express his continuing presence and healing of all human life, there was surely no better one than the continuing everyday life of the family.

Our trouble, probably, is that we still don't believe that God is serious about *this life* too. We somehow have gotten the idea that there is an isolated and antiseptic "spiritual" life somewhere which is freed from such things as enjoying (or surviving) a noisy family meal, working on an assembly line, welcoming the total personal joys of sex, paying bills, watching television or going to visit mother-in-law.

It is *everything* about the married couples that Christ makes a visible sign-sacrament of his creative-healing love: their freedom, intelligence, feelings, bodies, work, play and prayer. He enters these to transform their lives with his own vitality. He is not just hovering near husband and wife, putting divine "labels" on things that are really not all that good. Because their life touches everything in the world, God is constantly creating, re-creating, and healing the world through them.

He gives himself to each of the partners through the love of the other. The husband receives Christ on his wedding day, and every day thereafter, through the love of his wife; the wife receives the love of Christ in the love of her husband. Their marriage is not a private affair; it has become part of the visible saving work of Christ.

In the experience of giving love, they have an insight into Christ's will to give himself totally to all human beings. In the experience of being loved, they have a sign of the infinite love of the Spirit dwelling in them.

Healing

The strongest objection to this "idealistic" presentation of Christian marriage usually comes, understandably, from husbands and wives, either by outright statements or by wry smiles. (After one sermon on marriage, a long-time married lady was heard to remark, "I wish I knew as little about marriage as he does!") All well and good to speak "idealistically" of Eucharist, God's love, grace, Baptism, even confession. But when it comes to marriage — surely the experience of many couples bears out the fact that married life is so immersed in the not-so-merry-go-round of daily life, not to speak of its agony and despair, that to talk about husbands and wives beings signs of the love of Christ to the world is, well, extremely far-fetched.

Perhaps the priest-who-doesn't-know-anything-about-marriage may answer, "Baptism doesn't work miracles either, except the greatest miracle of all: the giving of God's life. It does not automatically produce a fully developed Christian, just as a baby's being born doesn't make him a fully developed person. He is born: now he must live. One family meal will mean its members are willing to *keep becoming a family*. The sacraments have not already wiped out all evil on earth; Christ is saving the world, and judging by externals alone, he has a long way to go. Men on earth have not yet grown to their full potential as human beings and Christians. That's what life is all about: growth and healing.

The sacrament of marriage is meant to be a sign of God's love for mankind and Christ's love for his Church. It is, like the Eucharist, a sign of the love that is already present and a sign of the love that is being created.

All marriages are somehow "sacraments" of God's love. Christian marriage is the concrete sign of Christ's revelation of God's love in everyday life.

If perfection were required before we dared receive the sacraments, there would really be no need for them! Christ would be putting a stamp of approval on what *we* have already achieved, a heretical thought at best. The sacramental signs of the Church, then, are signs of what Christ *is doing*. The pain, the struggle, the gaps in the love of husband and wife, the persistent selfishness, the failure to communicate—all these constitute precisely what Christ came to redeem. A Christian husband and wife are saying, by whatever faith they have: this life of ours is a sign, poor as it may be, of what Christ has done and is doing. This is as much as we have let him do, through us, and it's good. It may not seem like much, but it is the only hope the world has.

After such a "realistic" concession to the problems of marriage, we may dare to think of another aspect of the mystery of Christian marriage. "Mystery" is used here with something of the meaning of sacrament; it is something which reveals as well as hides. (Christ's incarnation reveals as well as "hides" God.)

Christian marriage is a sign, however imperfect, of the love of Father, Son and Spirit. In the mystery of the Trinity, the Father gives himself totally to the Son. This love is so great, this self-giving so total, that there is nothing of his being and perfection which he does not communicate to the Son. The Son, like the Father, is infinite God. The love that binds them is so rich that it gives expression to a Third Person who also is infinite God. None but a divine Person could express the depth and completeness of the love of Father and Son.

So the Christian family is a sign of God's inner life: the birth of a child proceeds from the total expression of mutual love between husband and wife. Their love is "personified," as it were, in their child, in his birth and his maturing.

The comparison is quite imperfect, of course. It is as far from the reality of God as man is from God. But it has a basis in truth. Christ enters their life—it is one of his signs—and places it within the whole mystery of salvation. The final purpose of marriage is the final purpose of all creation: that mankind be united in God forever.

The sacrament of marriage, therefore, is not something "over with" when the bride and groom leave the altar. It is not something like the flowers on the altar, beautiful for the occasion, but useless for the rest of life. Getting married and living married life is a sign of Christ's continuing presence in all life, creating and healing.

We are often reminded of the task of "building up" the Church. This implies that the Church itself is not yet what it can be, not just in the number of its people but in the quality of their love. Christ is, in the words of Paul, preparing his bride for the day when he will present her, "without spot or wrinkle," to the Father.

In a million little branch offices of the Kingdom, Christ is continuing his saving work. In a million homes where husband and wife struggle through their Passover together, Christ is organizing the great Passover of mankind to eternal freedom. In countless little churches, Christ is building up the "big" Church.

The Rite of Marriage

Liturgy of the Word
Exchange of vows
Exchange of rings
Profession of faith
Prayers of the faithful
Liturgy of the Eucharist
Nuptial blessing (after the Our Father)

Questions For Discussion

1. Do you think a truly loving marriage is a sign of God's relationship with human beings?
2. If your answer to No. 1 is yes, what is a truly loving Christian marriage a sign of? Can you name some concrete examples of this love being shown?
3. What does it mean to say that Jesus is the "marriage" of God and humanity?
4. Why is a lifelong commitment indispensable for a Christian marriage? Is it necessary for *any* marriage?
5. How might a family evaluate its success in "creating" persons — children, older relatives, neighbors, friends?
6. How does a family's continuing struggle to "keep becoming a family" help us understand the process of "building up the Church"?

Chapter XI

Holy Orders

Center of Unity

the Catholic Church is hierarchical, which to some people sounds like having an obscure virus. Moreover, the Catholic Church says Jesus wants it that way—the hierarchy, not the virus.

The dictionary defines "hierarchy" as "a ruling body of clergy organized into *orders* or ranks each subordinate to the one above it." The sacrament of "Holy Orders" has three major divisions: bishop, priest and deacon. What were formerly called "minor" orders are now called "ministries," such as those of acolyte and lector.

Although the *hierarchical* nature of the Catholic Church is not the only thing that distinguishes it from other churches, it is the source of most division and controversy. This fact, added to the increasing world-wide questioning of all authority, seems to require that we spend a little time examining the *organizational* side of the Church.

Even a quick reading of the New Testament reveals the fact that Jesus did designate twelve men to be something special, with Peter as at least the one who was to "confirm his brothers." He did send them to teach and proclaim a definite gospel. He did give them the responsibility (another word for authority) to represent his presence ("whoever hears you hears me"), to bind and loose, to feed the sheep. They are, as St. Irenaeus said in the second century: "teachers of doctrine, priests of sacred worship and officers of good order."

It could be said, of course, that the primary purpose of authority in the Church is to continue the tradition of Jesus' foot-washing and his giving his life for the sheep. This is as essential as the responsibility of making laws and condemning error. The problem is that even if a bishop wouldn't be caught dead washing somebody's feet, or a priest suffers less than anybody in this parish, there still have to be *centers of unity* around which the faithful gather. Jesus did not attempt the impossible task of forming a Body that has no parts, no organization of parts, or, what some would have, no *visible* parts. We may quarrel with the *style* of authority (too isolated, too centralized, too stern or too expensive) or even with the *abuse* of authority, but until we arrive at the only perfect democracy, a condition called heaven, we *members* of the Body will somehow have to work together by a system of joints and ligaments, a backbone and a head.

There is a distinction that is necessary, even if it sometimes turns into a divorce. A man (and many hope someday a woman) may have the power of *jurisdiction* and/or the power of *orders*. Perhaps the best way to explain this is to take a concrete example: Bishop Sheen is a bishop even if he is not the bishop guiding some particular diocese. Father Smith is a priest even if he is not in charge of a parish. Many people are surprised to find out that a priest may not preach or hear confessions (except in emergency, of course) unless he has the permission of the bishop of the diocese.

So the organization of "external" (if you'll pardon the expression) authority is one thing. Bishop John is the one who leads his people, whether he is a holy spirit or a holy terror. The organization of "internal" (if you'll pardon the expression) or spiritual authority is another. When Bishop Elderly takes part in Vatican II he continues the teaching office of the apostles even if he "has" no diocese. Father Wayout makes present the healing of Christ when he absolves a dying person even though the pastor had the police remove him from the pulpit and the bishop excommunicated and unfrocked him. The history of the Church shows that sometimes there is a Christlike combining of external structure and internal spirit, and sometimes there seems to be mere structure. The miracle promised by Christ is that the ship will never sink.

While we're on the subject of authority, we must rejoice in the fact that the laity are being called (and in many places allowed) to have their rightful place in the Church. They are not just to "pay and pray" but to have some "say."

Vatican II tells pastors to "recognize and promote the dignity as well as the responsibility of the layman in the Church. Let them willingly make use of his prudent advice. Let them confidently assign duties to him in the service of the Church, allowing him freedom and room for action. Further, let them encourage the layman so that he may undertake tasks on his own initiative. Attentively in Christ, let them consider with fatherly love the projects, suggestions, and desires proposed by the laity. Furthermore, let pastors respectfully acknowledge that just freedom which belongs to everyone in this earthly city" (Constitution on the Church, 37). While the language is guarded, and the English translation has no "she's," this statement is a further definition of authority.

The Three Orders

Before a more extensive consideration of the priesthood, which is the order Catholics are most familiar with, we should spell out the sacramental purpose of the episcopate and the diaconate.

Bishops. Vatican II says, "With their helpers, the priests and deacons, bishops have therefore taken up the service of the community, presiding in place of God over the flock whose shepherds they are, as teachers of doctrine, priests of sacred worship, and officers of good order. Just as the role that the Lord gave individually to Peter, the first among the apostles, is permanent and was meant to be transmitted to his successors, so also the apostles' office of nurturing the Church is permanent, and was meant to be exercised without interruption by the sacred order of bishops" (Constitution on the Church, 20).

"Episcopal consecration, together with the office of sanctifying, also confers the offices of teaching and of governing. (These, however, of their very nature, can be exercised only in hierarchical communion with the head and members of the college [that is, the Pope and the other bishops]). . . . Bishops in an eminent and visible way undertake Christ's role as Teacher,

Shepherd and High Priest, and they act in his person" (21).

"Among the principal duties of bishops, the preaching of the gospel occupies an eminent place" (25).

"Those chosen for the fullness of the priesthood are gifted with sacramental grace enabling them to exercise a perfect role of pastoral charity through prayer, sacrifice and preaching, as through every form of a bishop's care and service. They are enabled to lay down their life for their sheep fearlessly and, made a model for their flock, can lead the Church to an ever increasing holiness through their own example" (41).

Deacons. "At a lower level of the hierarchy are deacons, upon whom hands are imposed 'not unto the priesthood, but unto a ministry of service.' For strengthened by sacramental grace, in communion with the bishop and his group of priests, they serve the People of God in the ministry of the liturgy, of the word, and of charity. It is the duty of the deacon, to the extent that he has been authorized by competent authority, to administer baptism solemnly, to be custodian and dispenser of the Eucharist, to assist at and bless marriages in the name of the Church, to bring Viaticum to the dying, to read the sacred Scripture to the faithful, to instruct and exhort the people, to preside at the worship and prayer of the faithful, to administer sacramentals, and to officiate at funeral and burial services. Dedicated to duties of charity and of administration, let deacons be mindful of the admonition of Blessed Polycarp: 'Be merciful, diligent, walking according to the truth of the Lord, who became the servant of all.'

"These duties, so very necessary for the life of the Church, can in many areas be fulfilled only with difficulty according to the prevailing discipline of the Latin Church. For this reason, the diaconate can in the future be restored as a proper and permanent rank of the hierarchy. It pertains to the competent territorial bodies of bishops, of one kind or another, to decide, with the approval of the Supreme Pontiff, whether and where it is opportune for such deacons to be appointed for the care of souls. With the consent of the Roman Pontiff, this diaconate will be able to be conferred upon men of more mature age, even upon those living in the married state. It may also be conferred upon suitable young men. For them, however, the law of celibacy must remain intact" (29).

The permanent order of the diaconate was restored by Pope Paul in 1967, and has been introduced into a number of American dioceses.

The Priesthood

The Catholic priesthood today is caught between being too little and too much. There was a time when, in view of their almost limitless help to Catholic immigrants in the U.S., priests began to be placed on pedestals somewhat too high. On the other hand, the present "just call me Joe" atmosphere may raise a question as to any meaningful distinction between priest and lay person.

The "leftover laity," more than 99 per cent of the Church, are finally coming into their own. The baptismal priesthood, underemphasized because of Protestant rejection of the ministerial priesthood, is receiving increasing attention.

Still, Father cannot throw away his collar and sit in the pews. Or if he does, someone else will have to be *called* to the altar to be an individual sign of the presence of Christ the one priest.

Vatican II recognizes five "presences" of Christ in liturgical celebrations: 1) in the person of his minister; 2) under the Eucharistic species; 3) by his power, in the sacraments, "so that when a man baptizes it is really Christ himself who baptizes"; 4) in his word, "since it is he himself who speaks when the Holy Scriptures are read in the Church"; 5) finally, when the Church prays and sings, for he promised: "Where two or three are gathered together for my sake, there am I in the midst of them."

So, however you explain it, the priest has a special role in the Church, and is in a distinctive way a sign of the presence of Christ.

We have been insisting, throughout these chapters, that the great fact about the sacraments is that they are *visible*. The Christ who is always with us becomes visible in the sacramental actions of his Body. Eucharist is the clearest picture of the visible body of Christ.

As a center of unity, the priest is a visible assurance that God indeed does approach his people and offer them salvation. The priest is not a parish's attempt to "get to" God by electing a representative. He does represent in a special way the worship and faith of the people around the altar, just as Jesus is our Brother leading us to the Father. But Jesus is also God become incarnate to offer us his healing love; so also the priest is God's visible

offer of salvation and an assurance that he wishes to gather his children around him. If the Church is a sign lifted up among the nations so that they can see the light of Christ, the priest is the visible center where the Christians can gather to lift the sign.

All this can be very embarrassing for ultra-democratic advocates of equality. Why should one man—any man—be considered "special"? He doesn't necessarily know more than others; he isn't necessarily any holier; his experience of life may be rather narrow, or at least not as mundane as that of his parishioners; he may even exhibit some of the same immaturity as the rest of men. What, then, is the source of his being "special"?

The answer is, of course, Christ.

There is a dramatic ceremony sometimes connected with the ordination of a priest. After the ordaining bishop has conferred the sacrament by silently placing his hands on the head of the one to be ordained, all the priests who are present file past the newly-ordained priest and also press their hands down on his head. It is a vivid reminder of the fact that there is only one priesthood; that through the bishop priests are linked to the apostles, and through them to the One Priest, Jesus Christ.

Man does not save his soul by his own efforts. The Church is not a sign lifted up among the nations and drawing all men to itself by the brilliance of its philosophers and theologians, the skill of its ad men or the organization of a worldwide communications network. Not that the Church should neglect any human art or science in its witness to the world. But the Light—the only Light—is Christ.

He shines in poor lanterns often, whether they be priests or laymen. But he does shine. And this is the tremendous assurance of the sacraments, in this case, the priesthood. This man, taken from among the men he leads, is Christ's visible assurance that he is present and acting. When the Church assembles for the Eucharist, it is not a human attempt to reach God: it is God declaring visibly that he joins them into one, forgives and nourishes them. It does matter, humanly, which priest is the "president of the assembly"; but God can use even a poor instrument.

It is God's greatest tribute to the dignity of his creature that he puts the *most precious value in the world into his care: the Body of Christ.* And he manages, even while leaving man free, to have his "way," his "will," i.e., of having his love possess the heart of man.

The poorest priest, morally, intellectually, physically, in the poorest church in the world is an absolutely valid assurance that Christ's healing power is there. The worst sinner, the most agonized sufferer, the most doubting Thomas can look at the altar and be absolutely certain that the offer of salvation is indeed "near."

All this is not to say that most priests cut a poor figure humanly. The sometimes overwhelming honor that Catholic people give their priests is testimony to the zeal and holiness with which they have been served. But just in case this is not so, Christ says, I am *still* there.

What is the primary purpose of the priest, then? He is the visible center of unity in the Church.

Christ's whole purpose in coming was that we be one in charity—*and visibly so;* his twelve apostles were to be the official witnesses of his life, death and resurrection, the definitive proclaimers of his word, the representers of his priestly sacrifice; the builders of a visible-invisible Church.

It is not surprising, then, that Vatican II states that priests constitute one priesthood with the bishop. "Priests make him [the bishop] present, in a certain sense, in the individual local congregations of the faithful" (Constitution on the Church, 28).

Always unity, then. But not mere physical, external unity. The priest is to build up the community of love, continuing the primary purpose for which Christ came.

We are back, again, to the Church community as sacrament of Christ. The *community* is the first sacrament that the world (and the Church itself) sees. If this group is not a sign of Christ, we must say again that its individual seven signs may be meaningless to most people.

The priest is at the service of the community. He is not a priest for himself. It is noteworthy that the revised ritual for ordination published by Pope Paul in 1968, advises priests and deacons to ordinarily be ordained in the local church (or at least the diocese) in which they will serve. It will be somewhat a surprise for many Catholics to learn that the same ritual calls for the active consent of the congregation to this man's being ordained.

The instruction of the bishop identifies three works of a priest, each aimed at the good of the whole community. The new priest is reminded that he continues the work of *Christ the Teacher*. The priest is not some kind of undefinable center of a misty "spiritual" Church. He represents Christ, who did *do* definite and identifiable things and who did *say* definite and definable words. So there is an essential message to be spoken in the Church, and this proclamation of the Good News is one of the primary functions of the priest. He is a "prophet," speaking the definite word of Christ.

There are other "prophets" that rise in the Church, sometimes to challenge and even purify the proclamations of the official witnesses of Christ. This is good and healthy. But the official proclaimers remain.

Today, many people complain that priests will no longer give them "answers" as they used to do. They are not "definite" about what one should do to be a good Christian. This is not necessarily a defaulting of priestly proclamation of the gospel. It has simply become evident that "counseling" is not "telling people what to do," but helping them realize their feelings and come to a mature decision of their own.

Most of the time this has to do with concrete situations where only the individual involved can make the decision. It is not the business of the priest to decide when his parishioners should pray, or take a vacation; it is not within his competence to tell them when a hysterectomy is advisable, or when they, in their individual circumstances, may practice rhythm. His purpose is to proclaim the Good News as Christ did: the principles of the Gospel, the events of Jesus' life, the activity of Christ in the world today.

It may be, indeed, that in our preoccupation with

particular problems, and in the flood of complexity that has overwhelmed us, we may think that the Church, in its priests, is not "telling us what to do" with sufficient clarity. But the fact may be that the essentials are being proclaimed in a better way than before, in the new emphasis on the primary fact of Christianity, love of God and neighbor. On the other hand, there is a vast body of gospel proclamation contained in the documents of Vatican II that should be "direction" enough for a long time to come.

The second part of the bishop's instruction in the new ritual speaks of *Christ the Priest*. The new priest is to make his own the mission of making the world holy in Christ. He joins the spiritual sacrifices of the faithful to the eucharistic sacrifice of Christ.

Christ's presence does not become visible merely in bread and wine, but also in the priest himself.

Christ is of course present wherever "two or three are gathered together in my name." But the unique gathering together to celebrate the Eucharist requires the presence of one who visibly takes the place of the "great high priest who has passed through the heavens," and is no longer visible as he was in his mortal life.

The "center-ness" of Christ is made visible through the priest: the fact that Christ is Head, Source, Leader, Servant, Shepherd. Every Christian re-presents Christ to the world, as the one who brings healing, forgiveness, love. The priest's distinct office is that he is the sacrament of Christ as Head of the Body.

Vatican II says, "[Priests] exercise the sacred function of Christ most of all in the Eucharistic liturgy. There, acting in the person of Christ and proclaiming his mystery, they join the offering of the faithful to the sacrifice of their Head. Until the coming of the Lord they re-present and apply in the sacrifice of the Mass, the one sacrifice of Christ offering himself once and for all to the Father as a spotless victim" (Constitution on the Church, 28).

Thus, the community that stands about the Eucharistic altar in faith and love can be absolutely certain, not ever forgetting their faults, that they are worshipping in a way that pleases the Father, because they are obeying the instruction of Christ, "Do this in memory of me." They can be certain that, in this man whom Christ has chosen, they have the instrument of the perfect priesthood of Christ. The homage they can pay to God is perfect; perfect, also, is the assurance that this sacrifice is pleasing to the Father, that he accepts their offering and continues his offer of friendship.

Finally, the bishop reminds the candidate that his work is that of *Christ the Pastor*. "Pastor," of course, means "shepherd," and the priest's model is obviously the Good Shepherd.

"Sheep" is not an "in" word in a personalistic and individualistic world. The priest is not to ask the people for mindless or childish obedience: he wouldn't get it anyway today. His job as shepherd is to show the way—to do himself the believing, loving, praying, fasting, serving. Like the Good Shepherd, he must know his people, *their* everyday experiences and problems, *their* world and values and needs. Indeed, the word "pastoral" as applied to theology seems to have acquired the meaning of "realistic." A "pastoral" decision does not set principles aside: it tempers the wind to the shorn lamb, as it were.

Priests are pastoral (even when they may still be languishing as "assistant pastors") when they are primarily concerned with giving their lives for the "sheep," highly educated sheep, cantankerous ones, bored, rebellious, ignorant, pushy, simple, mystical ones. His job is to carry the erring (as he will often be carried himself) on shoulders of compassion, patience and hope.

It is obvious that Christ did not define—could not have defined—the many pastoral activities and structures that have developed in the organization of the Church over the centuries and which are still subject to the changing needs of the people of God: the manifold activities of the pope, the immense, delegated power exercised by the Roman Curia, the international structure of nuncios and legates, the canonical particulars of dioceses and parishes. But the essentials—Peter and the apostles, the ministerial priesthood—these were there from the beginning.

The problem is that the structure which is essential to any continuing human activity sometimes gets overlaid with the culture of a period, with the personal idiosyncracies of those who make it visible. The structure itself—priesthood—is sometimes hampered by the "structure" into which it must enter—the individual priest.

There is only one test by which any community can ultimately be judged truly worthy to be called the Church of Christ: "By this will all men know that you are my disciples, if you have love one for another." The priest is not a mere functionary. His ultimate purpose is the same as the purpose of the incarnation of Christ the Priest: visibly to mediate God's love to and from the hearts of men. His sermons must not be mere information, but a means of reconciling the people before him to God and to each other. His parish "plant" is not a monument to successful financing, but a sign that men can come together in peace. His theology must be a light to people who find it hard to forgive their neighbor or even themselves.

A priest offers Mass so that men may love one another as Christ loves them, and show it by their joining together in worship. "I have come that you may be one." No matter what differences of opinion may churn within a community, there is a person around whom the members can unite in basic agreement of heart and faith. The priest—*some* priest, *any* priest—is the center of unity around whom they must unite, if they are to sit at the one Table.

The Rite of Ordination to the Priesthood

Liturgy of the Word
Choosing of candidates—official approval
Consent of the people (e.g., by applause)
Bishop's instruction
Examination of candidates
Promise of obedience to the bishop
Invitation to prayer
Laying on of hands
Prayer of consecration

Investiture with priest's stole and chasuble
Anointing of hands
Presentation of paten with bread and chalice with
    wine and water
Kiss of peace
Eucharist: first Mass of newly ordained

Questions For Discussion

1. One of the "presences" of Christ is in the priest at
    Mass. Does this depend on the holiness of the
    priest?
2. Should a priest be "one of the boys"? Where do
    the laity draw the line?
3. What is the difference between the priest's "pro-
    claiming the gospel," "teaching" religion, and
    inevitably expressing his own opinions and per-
    sonality?
4. What do you expect of the priest at Mass, apart
    from the homily? Does he pray instead of you,
    or as your representative, or as a fellow Chris-
    tian?
5. What are the most "pastoral" things priests have
    done for you?

Chapter XII

Baptism

Infant Baptism:
A Birthday and a Promise

the Eucharistic community, around its priest, together with a "little church," celebrates the Christ-ing of a new member by Baptism.

For most of us, Baptism is not a great dramatic moment of adult life. We don't see ourselves as having been thrown into a hopeless world, wandering about in black despair, then "discovering" Christ and deciding to follow him. We might appreciate our relationship more deeply if that were the case, but we might also suffer some terrible scars in the process, and we might even miss him altogether.

Rather, God prefers growth that is gradual and as peaceful as possible. He doesn't create twenty-one-year-old college graduates, or century-old sequoias. He makes life to be given and received, and if this doesn't happen, there isn't any life.

For most of us the Christian life is something given us as babies by two communities: our family and our Church. The Big Church, the community of Christ, is already there, waiting to give us a place at

its table; the Little Church is already there, in our father and mother. They welcome us into their own
community. They promise such good example that
the little person's gradual growth to conscious and
free commitment to Christ will seem almost "natural."

The two communities lead us from complete helplessness to a full and adult commitment to life in
Christ. For as long as we need, we grow in the
warmth of this womb of Christian-human life. As
soon as we can, we take our adult place at the table of
Christ and the table of life.

The question of infant Baptism is a perennial one.
Some take the position that only an adult can make
the total Christian decision—which is true—and
therefore that babies should not be baptized—which
is a different matter.

The new rite for the Christian Initiation of
Adults, which will be discussed in the next chapter,
obviously requires a deeply experienced and serious
decision on the part of the adult candidate for Baptism. But this ritual is intended to be used for those
who do not know Christ at all.

But what of the children reared in the hundreds
of millions of Christian homes in the world, or the
claimed 60-plus million Christian homes in the United States? Can they be raised in a *Christian* home and
kept antiseptically free from all Christian influence,
supposing for the moment that this is possible? And if
there is to be no Christian influence, what is the sub-
stitute? Judaism? Hinduism? Paganism? Hedonism?
Atheism? Can anyone seriously propose that Christian parents—truly Christian parents, of course—

could do anything but try their best to show their children such a dedicated Christian life that they would gradually grow into such commitment themselves?

There is no such thing as being neutral—morally or humanly. Questions of right or wrong, justice and responsibility, arise in the worst and the best of circumstances. *Children are always being taught the values of their parents.* If the values of their parents are to have no values, that's what the children learn. It seems cruel (apart from its being impossible) to advocate to any parents—Christian, Jewish, Moslem—that they let their children wander through childhood and adolescence in a moral desert and expect them, at 18 or 21, to have the moral courage to make a fundamental religious decision.

Are there not some essential obligations that predate anyone's life? The values of almost all cultures require that no one inflict cruelty on another, or violate his person; most of us agree that murder, robbery, rape, arson, slander are not a matter of choice. They are wrong, and we feel perfectly justified in teaching the values involved to our children, as soon and as well as possible. We don't feel that one should be allowed to wait until he is twenty-one before deciding whether or not it is good to be a member of Murder Incorporated.

He may in fact decide to become a murderer. If we discover that decision with reasonable probability, we stop his external action. In short, we don't feel we are "imposing" any unwarranted obligations on him when we teach him from the beginning that human life must be respected.

Even more simply: Surely no parent in the world feels it is unfair to a little girl to teach her from the beginning to bathe, to eat properly, to rest, to learn about life. These are essential values to the parents who would be neglectful if they did not attempt seriously to give these values to their children. Actually, it's not a question *whether* or not to impart values to a child. If a child doesn't absorb them from parents, he will absorb them from someone else—his peers, TV, teachers, society at large. The question is, therefore, *which values* to impart, and a parent who loves a child will want to give none but the highest.

Can the Christian life be compared to these essential values? For Christian parents it is the highest value of all. *They are absolutely sure* that this is the greatest goodness they can give their children. Hence it is only logical for the Church, out of its own faith, to want its children to be fully incorporated into the Christian life at the very beginning of their growth to complete personhood.

Some will still object that parents can give children all this inspiration and training without having them actually baptized. How can anyone receive a sacrament if he or she is not able to make a conscious and free decision?

The answer of those Christian churches who practice infant Baptism is that sacraments are not *isolated* events in our lives, but the visible sign of *divine and human* activity that covers our whole life. Even the most ardent adult convert from paganism has a lot to learn and a long way to go. Bride and groom intend to live happily ever after, but they will learn, if they

do not already have the wisdom to know, that mature marital relationships do not spring full-blown from the honeymoon. Similarly, going to confession is one manifestation of a lifelong process of conversion.

So the baby is baptized under the presumption that he or she will be raised in a Christian atmosphere of family and parish. If there is no hope of this, the baby may not be baptized.

But supposing the Christian example the baby will receive, the only answer to the question of infant Baptism is "Why not?"

A word should be said here about infants who die without Baptism. We are dealing with the unknown here. Does anyone suppose that a *baptized* baby who dies will remain a baby forever? Well then, how does the baby "grow up" to mature love of God after its death? We should learn to say more frequently and easily, "We just don't know. God does all things wisely, and he will do this perfectly, without taking away the freedom of the person."

Now, if God wills the salvation of *all* persons (even though none of us has a right to divine life), will he not give the unbaptized baby the same opportunity to love him maturely as he gives the baptized baby?

We are therefore brought to the conclusion that the baby is baptized not in view of its possible imminent death but in view of a whole lifetime. Convinced Christians want the process *and the sign* of God's making us his children to begin as soon as possible. The baptized baby is already holy in its *being*; parents and Church now begin the task of leading the little person to be holy by *choice*.

But perhaps there is a deeper reason for infant

Baptism, one that can easily be joined to the foregoing. The reason is that the Christian life is absolutely the gift of God. It is not something an adult man or woman can "work" themselves into. It is not like becoming a good lawyer, or fashion designer, or golfer; here practice makes perfect, genius is 99 per cent hard work. But the Christian life is something that only God can give; it is subject to no human meriting. It is not even subject to human reasoning. A man must indeed act rationally; he must choose truth and goodness. But the heart of the Christian life is that God loves us first; we are entirely his creatures.

When the Christian mother and father bring their baby to the Christian community and ask for Baptism, then, they are making a public profession of the grace-filled essence of the Christian life. They are saying, implicitly, "Only Christ can give this baby his life; through the Sacrament of Christ, his Church, this baby can be made a living member of Christ. It is not a human achievement; it is not something for us to 'give' or 'withhold.' Our own relationship with Christ tells us that the greatest thing we can do for our child is to love him within the sacrament of our own home and the sacrament of Eucharistic Christian life."

And thus, because of faith-full Christian parents, most of us were given membership in Christ almost as soon as we were born, and over the years we were given all the visible (sacramental) helps of the Little Church and the Big Church to help us freely and consciously come to adult Christian life.

Baptism is a sign that God is making it possible

for us to live his life, as children and as adults, in this life and forever. Whether we are speaking of infant Baptism or adult Baptism, the primary statement is, "This is what Christ is doing for me." Only secondarily is it a statement that "I decide for Christ. I accept Christ totally."

The Rite of Infant Baptism

Greeting and welcome
Signing of forehead of child by priest and community
Scriptural readings and homily
Prayer of the faithful
Prayer of exorcism
Anointing
Renunciation of sin, profession of faith (parents and
 godparents)
Baptism
Anointing with chrism
Clothing with white garment
Lighted candle
Procession to the altar, song
Lord's Prayer
Blessing

Questions For Discussion

1. What do you think would happen in a family that tried to be completely neutral on all moral and religious questions?
2. Why is it essential to emphasize Baptism as "what Christ is doing for me" rather than "what

I am doing for Christ"?

3. What does it mean to say that our whole life is a baptismal dying and rising? Name an instance of your Christian "dying" today? What was the "rising" that followed?

4. How do the Little Church (the family) and the Big Church work together in the formation of mature Christians?

5. What are some occasions when Christians baptized as babies come to a deeper commitment to Christ?

Chapter XIII

Baptism

Adult Baptism:
Model For Conversion

the act of faith is a decision, at the core of my being, to be filled with the spirit of Christ in my whole life.

Is this a decision that is made at one particular moment—as in the case of an adult conversion from, say, paganism or from a life of serious sinfulness—or is it a decision that grows so imperceptibly that it is difficult to say exactly just when it became fully adult and basic? To ask the question is to give the answer. Our experience seems to indicate that both alternatives are actual.

In any case, every Christian is called to a full conversion to Christ, an absolute acceptance of him as the source and center and model of all life, the way to the Father, and to rebirth in his Spirit.

We will never solve the mystery of the tension between the need for a once-and-for-all decision and the incompleteness of human life. Hence it is necessary for all of us (for ourselves and as parents of children) to be aware of the constant call of God to *ratify* our Baptism. Each Eucharistic celebration is in a sense a public avowal that we *do* want to make a full baptismal commitment. It is willingness to be completed in all that is lacking: it is something continuing and growing, even while it is attempting to be basic and absolute.

One form of the baptismal rite in the early Church provides us with a vivid dramatic portrayal of what we are about: *dying and rising in Christ.*

The one to be baptized comes to the community after long preparation. Near the pool which will symbolize his death and resurrection, he is welcomed. He professes his faith; the assembled Church prays for him; the devil is exorcized; the whole body of the new Christian is anointed with oil as a sign of purification. Finally he is led by a priest or deacon—or, in the case of a woman, by a woman, in a separate baptismal pool—down the steps into the water. The Church, assembled around and acting through a representative, constitutes a sacrament of rebirth in Christ. The catechumen is gently lowered beneath the surface of the water. Apparently he is gone, dead; whatever he was has disappeared. Whatever was his achievement or his sin, his independence or his misery, is gone. This is an end and a beginning.

Then the word is spoken: "I baptize you in the name of the Father and of the Son and of the Holy Spirit." With Christ holding him by the hand, the man is raised up out of the water—death, nothingness—into a new life. He walks up the steps on the other side of the pool as a new creation. He has been born into a life that is beyond the human but joined to the human: divine life in human nature. He is a member of Christ. He is anointed again, now in dignity and priesthood with Christ.

It is this ceremony that St. Paul was undoubtedly referring to when he wrote: "When we were baptized in Christ Jesus we were baptized in his death; . . . we went into the tomb with him and joined him in death, so that as he was raised from the dead by the Father's glory (i.e., power), we too might live a new life. . . .Our former selves have been crucified with him . . . to free us from the slavery of sin. When he died, he died, once and for all, to sin, so that his life now is life with God; in that way you too must consider yourselves to be dead to sin but alive for God in Christ Jesus" (Romans 6:3ff).

Our life is a baptismal dying and rising. Christ comes to us in the Sacrament of the Church, the community of those who have received his life and who show his presence visibly in the world. The Church asks me, "What do you desire?" I reply, "Faith"—that is, the complete surrender of my person to this God coming to me with his offer; the complete assent of my mind to the word and action whereby he communicates his life to me. And because Christ has already given me the ability to say this word, the visible Church takes me to the sacramental birth of water and the Spirit. In the waters of the new Jordan I am Christ going down, coming up to new life; in the new Red Sea I escape with the people of God from the slavery of sin, Satan and death, and I walk in new freedom. In a new Calvary of total turning to the Father, I am plunged into Christ's death; in a new Easter my Father raises me up in Christ. I am born again. It is not a repetition of my first birth; it is not a metaphorical rebirth, like turning over a new moral leaf: I am literally raised to a new plane of being. I belong to the communion called Christ's Body. His life, his love, his light possess me: I am "in" the Kingdom of the Father.

The New Rite of Adult Initiation

We come now to what liturgists have called one of the most "revolutionary" changes the Church has made for a long time. It is the new rite for the Christian Initiation of Adults.

In the previous chapter we discussed the importance of infant Baptism of babies *born into Christian homes*, and we saw that, even though the world is only 30 per cent Christian, there will be plenty of occasions for this celebration.

But the world *is* 70 per cent non-Christian, and the Church's business is to proclaim the Good News to that great multitude. For those who become interested, the Church has the task of leading them gradually to a *truly* Christian choice.

In the words of a respected liturgist, Ralph Keifer, the new rite which Pope Paul approved in 1972 *"reverses a thousand years of practice and attitudes. . . . The primary rites of initiation . . . have been turned upside down and inside out, heralding a summons to begin the most radical sort of reform and renewal. . . . And this change has gone unnoticed, virtually without comment and with scarcely a word of dissent."*

Father Aidan Kavanaugh, O.S.B., director of the graduate program in liturgy at Notre Dame, has this to say, "This document may well appear to a writer a century from now as the most important result of the Second Vatican Council for the life of the Church."

What's going on here?

The most obvious feature of the new rite is the restoration of one of the features of early Christianity —the *catechumenate* (from the Greek word which means "to teach"). This involves an extended period of preparation and training of "catechumens," those who belong to a special order in the Church and are publicly and officially on their way to being incorporated into the Church. The new rite calls for a very serious approach—no six- or eight-week catechism course. It involves, insofar as this is possible to human ministry the making of real Christians. The length of this period of preparation will vary according to circumstances.

But one must say that the greatest effect will be felt by those of us who have been born into the Church and have always considered ourselves full-fledged Christians.

We're in for a shock.

We are going to be forced to ask ourselves, "If this is what it means to be a Christian, where in the world am I?"

Much of the following is simply quoted from the new ritual. Emphasis is added to show the part to be played by those of us who already *are* the Church, for better or for worse.

The new rite explains: "The initiation of the catechumens takes place step-by-step *in the midst of the community of the faithful*. Together with the catechumens, *the faithful* reflect upon the value of the paschal mystery, *renew their own conversion,* and *by their example* lead the catechumens to obey the Holy Spirit more generously."

Four Stages of Initiation

The process of becoming Christian comprises four steps. First, the *pre-catechumenate;* then the *catechumenate,* which may last for several years; third, the *Lenten preparation;* finally, the *Easter celebration* and the following seven weeks.

1. The *pre-catechumenate* is a time when "the living God is proclaimed, as in Jesus Christ. . . . Thus those who are not yet Christians, their hearts opened by the Holy Spirit, may believe and be freely converted to the Lord. . . . From evangelization, conducted with the help of God, come faith and initial conversion, by which each one feels himself called away from sin and drawn toward the mystery of God's love. . . . During this time catechists, deacons and priests *as well as lay persons,* suitably explain the Gospel to the candidates."

2. The *catechumenate* begins with formal entrance into the order and ends with the day of "election," that is, of being chosen for Baptism by the Church. After this ceremony, the converts-to-be are considered members of the Church. "Helped by the example and support of sponsors and godparents *and the whole community of the faithful,* the catechumens will learn to pray to God more easily, to witness to the faith, to be constant in the expectation of Christ in all things, to follow supernatural inspiration in their actions, and to exercise charity toward neighbors to the point of self-renunciation."

It looks as though we're all in for some re-formation! What will we think when "Ordinarily, when they are present *in the assembly of the faithful*, they should be dismissed in a friendly manner before the eucharistic celebration begins, unless there are difficulties." There *will* be difficulties, not on the part of the catechumens, but in the consciences of us who remain for the Eucharist, presumably because we have come to be full-fledged Christians!

3. Lent for the catechumens is the period of "purification and enlightenment." "Lent is a memorial or a preparation for Baptism and a time" of penance. *It renews the community of the faithful* together with the catechumens and makes them ready to celebrate the paschal mystery which the sacraments of initiation apply to each individual."

During this time the Church makes the "election," that is, the choice and admission of the catechumens for Baptism at Easter. "The admission made by the Church is founded in the election by God, in whose name the Church acts.

"Before the election is celebrated, the candidates are expected to have a conversion of mind and morals, a sufficient knowledge of Christian teaching, and a sense of faith and charity; . . . the manifestation of their intention and the decision of the bishop or his delegate should take place *in the presence of the community*.

"During this period, a more intense preparation of the mind, which involves spiritual recollection more than catechesis, is intended to purify their minds and hearts by the examination of conscience

127

and by repentance, and to enlighten their minds and hearts by a deeper knowledge of Christ the savior. This is done especially in the so-called 'scrutinies' and 'presentations.' "

The scrutinies are held in church on the third, fourth and fifth Sundays of Lent (readings from cycle A are used). They consist of silent and public prayer, and exorcism. "The purpose is mainly spiritual, to purify the catechumens' minds and hearts, to strengthen them against temptation, to purify their intentions and to make firm their decision."

The presentations are the handing over to these "elect" the ancient documents of faith and prayer (the Creed and the Our Father).

4. Initiation and the Easter season are the climax of months or years of preparation. At the great celebration at the Easter Vigil, the catechumens are baptized, confirmed and celebrate the Eucharist for the first time. The whole Easter season is a time for deepening their Christian experience and entering more closely into the life of the community of the faithful.

The Sacraments of Intitiation

It may come as a surprise to some that there are three sacraments of initiation, not one: Baptism-Confirmation-Eucharist, and they are to be celebrated on the same occasion. The proper time for this celebration is the Easter Vigil, Holy Saturday night.

Baptism. The ritual has some pointed words here (again, it is the rest of the faithful who are going to be more challenged) in connection with becoming a Christian. "Adults are not saved unless they come forward of their own accord and are willing to accept the gift of God by faith. Baptism is the sacrament of faith, not only the faith of the Church, but also the candidates' own faith; and it is expected that it will be an active faith in them. When they are baptized, they should not receive such a sacrament passively, for of their own will they enter into a covenant with Christ, rejecting their errors and adhering to the true God.

As for the baptismal ceremony itself: "The washing with water is a sign of mystical sharing in the death and rising of Christ, by which *believers* in his name die to sin and rise to eternal life. . . . The washing is not merely a rite of purification but a sacrament of union with Christ."

Confirmation. "According to the ancient practice maintained in the Roman liturgy, an adult is not to be baptized unless he receives Confirmation immediately afterward, provided no serious obstacles exist. This connection signifies the unity of the paschal mystery, the close relationship between the mission of the Son and the pouring out of the Holy Spirit, and the joint celebration of the sacraments by which the Son and the Spirit come with the Father upon those who are baptized."

First Sharing in the Eucharist. "Finally the Eucharist is celebrated, and for the first time the neophytes (newly brought forth) have the full right to take part. This is the culminating point of their initiation. In the Eucharist, the neophytes who have received the dignity of royal priesthood have an active part in the general intercessions (Prayer of the Faithful) and, as far as possible, in the rite of bringing the offerings to the altar. With the whole community they take part in the action of the sacrifice, and they say the Lord's Prayer, thus showing the spirit of adoption as God's children which they have received in Baptism. Then, by receiving the body that was handed over and the blood that was shed, they confirm the gifts they have received and acquire a foretaste of eternal things."

Period of Post-Baptismal Catechesis

"The *community* and neophytes move forward together, meditating on the Gospel, sharing in the Eucharist and performing works of charity. . . . *They* have been renewed in mind, have tasted more intimately the good word of God, have shared in the Holy Spirit and have come to discover the goodness of the Lord. From this experience which is proper to the Christian and is increased by the way he lives, *they* draw a new sense of the faith, the Church, and the world."

The occasion for this post-baptismal catechesis will be the Sunday Masses of the Easter season. We may now notice that the readings have a very definite orientation to the newly baptized, especially those of cycle A. "*The whole local community* should be invited to these Masses."

What's a Born Catholic to Do?

It should be evident, as was said above, that all of us baptized as infants are going to be mightily challenged if the new rite is carried out in our parishes as it should be. Three observations seem to be in order.

First, all of us are presumed to have grown into an appreciation of what our baptized condition centers on: the dying and rising of Christ, to be mirrored in our lives every day. We are baptized into the risen Christ and the indwelling Spirit.

Second, our baptismal life is something to be experienced, not just theoretically known. Faith is not something merely in our minds; it is a way of living together in Jesus Christ. Baptism is the outcome of real and radical conversion. The Passover mystery of Jesus' death and resurrection is first of all an event and an experience, and only secondly a doctrine. We are to experience God's works occurring amongst us.

Third, the new rite challenges us as a community to be a real community. The new Christians learn by sharing our experience. If we are a Church that is an "it," just an institution, and not a faith community, then the new rite will never get off the ground. It is the *community* that accompanies the catechumen all the way to Baptism. It will succeed only if we are all ready to be challenged by his conversion and use it as an occasion for a greater faithfulness to Christ on our part. It is an incongruity to welcome people into a "community" of strangers. Shaping, training, forming people to live as Christians is the Church's highest priority. On the other hand, the catechumens are ministers too—their experience of transformation witnesses to us the power of Christ, the risen Lord.

Baptism calls for a radical transformation of life and values that is publicly celebrated as the responsibility of the whole body of Christ, the Church. The new rite challenges every one of us to ask ourselves to what degree our faith is radical—at the roots of our life—and how much it is merely implicit, absorbed through a Christian culture of home and Church and mixed with American, naturalistic and other values.

131

The Rite of Christian Initiation for Adults

1. *Precatechumenate.* Inquiry, evangelization.
2. *Catechumenate.* Complete catechesis, entrance into the order of catechumens, period of training, election
3. *Purification and Enlightenment: Lent.* Scrutinies on Sundays of Lent, presentation of Creed and Lord's Prayer, Christian name
4. *Celebration of the Sacraments of Initiation: Easter Vigil*
   a) *Baptism:* Instruction, litany, renunciation, anointing, profession of faith, Baptism (by immersion, infusion or pouring), clothing with white garment, presentation of lighted candle
   b) *Confirmation:* Prayer, anointing
   c) *Eucharist*
5. *Post-Baptismal Catechesis.* Sunday Masses during the seven weeks of the Easter season

These two chapters have discussed the sacraments of *initiation.* If one has already been validly initiated, it is obviously impossible to repeat the process. Therefore the Church has a ritual for receiving "into full communion with the Catholic Church" those who are already Christians and have been members of a Protestant or Orthodox Church.

The Rite of Reception of Baptized Christians Into Full Communion With the Catholic Church

Liturgy of the Word.

Homily
Invitation to profession of faith
Community recitation of the creed
Personal profession of faith
Confirmation (or imposition of hands)
Sign of peace
Prayers of the Faithful
Liturgy of the Eucharist

Questions For Discussion

1. Why isn't it enough to be simply a "private" Christian, loving Christ as an individual, not bothering with a "community"?

2. Which better symbolizes the meaning of Baptism for you: immersion (as in the baptismal pool) or pouring of water on your forehead?

3. What activities in the childhood, adolescence and adulthood of born Catholics would correspond to the catechumenate?

4. How do you see the whole program carried out in your parish? How many catechumens would be needed? Would they be embarrassed? Would you?

5. Why should 14 weeks of the Church year (six of Lent and eight after Easter) be specially dedicated to forming new Christians and re-forming old ones?

Chapter XIV

Confirmation

"Let Your Light Shine Before Men"

"**b**e *sealed with the Gift of the Holy Spirit*" (Confirmation formula from the new ritual, revised by the Congregation for Divine Worship and approved by Pope Paul, August 15, 1971).

The same Father, the same Lord Jesus, *and the same Holy Spirit* pour out the full force of divine love for us 24 hours a day. God loves all of us all the time with a love we cannot even imagine.

At certain peak moments this love is made *reassuringly visible* in the acts of Christ in his Church—which we call sacraments. Obviously we do not get a "different" God with each sacramental celebration. The differences of the sacraments have to do with us, not with God. Each of them is addressed to a special, or distinctive, situation in *our* lives. So, there are seven sacraments, a sevenfold articulation of the one word of grace.

But it is also true to say that there is only one "primordial" sacrament who is Christ, and only one fundamental sacrament, the Church. The seven sacraments are not isolated events in a profane life; rather, they are its innermost life.

All this is said to lay the foundations for answering some persistent questions about Confirmation. How can we say that we "receive" the Holy Spirit in Confirmation when this has already happened in Baptism? How can there be "more" of the Holy Spirit—as if God held back a little in the first sacrament?

A simple, and hopefully not a simplistic, answer is: At Confirmation Jesus repeats, as it were, what he said at our Baptism: "Your light must shine before men so that they may see goodness in your acts and give praise to your heavenly Father" and "You will receive power when the Holy Spirit comes down on you [*for the special purpose of being*] my witnesses in Jerusalem, throughout Judea and Samaria, yes, even to the ends of the earth."

The difficulty (for those who find one) stems from the fact that Baptism and Confirmation were celebrated together, along with Eucharist, in the early Church. Now that all three sacraments of initiation are to be celebrated together for adults, perhaps the question about receiving the Holy Spirit "again" will go away. When Baptism and Confirmation were celebrated at different times, the communication of the Holy Spirit fundamentally in Baptism remained, so to speak, in the background.

Perhaps a comparison of Easter with Pentecost will help. The second is implicit in the first.

In fact, according to St. John (20:19-23), Jesus breathed his Holy Spirit on his apostles in an appearance on Easter day itself, and sent them into the world. Matthew implies some time between the resurrection and the appearance of Jesus in Galilee. Luke, of course, is the source of the 50-day interval. But the Gospel writers did not primarily concern themselves with calendars and geography, and neither should we. The point is that Jesus not only rose by the power of the Spirit to new life in the presence of the Father (a symbol of our Baptism); he also became, with the Father, the bestower of the Holy Spirit upon all mankind (our Baptism and, for the purpose of witness, our Confirmation). Pentecost has a meaning of its own, even though it is derived from Good Friday and Easter.

Father Aidan Kavanaugh, writing in *Worship* (48:6, p. 328), quotes the new ritual for adult Baptism and comments: "According to the ancient practice maintained in the Roman liturgy, an adult is not to be baptized unless he receives Confirmation immediately afterward, provided no serious obstacles exist. *This connection signifies the unity of the paschal mystery, the close relationship between the mission of the Son and the pouring out of the Holy Spirit, and the joint celebration of the sacraments by which the Son and the Spirit come with the Father upon those who are baptized* [34; emphasis added].

"The theological point made here is of such seriousness that one feels compelled to ask why and how it can be construed as applying only to adults and not to infants and children, especially if they are baptized at the Easter vigil. Unless the theological point is dismissed as mere rhetoric, it seems inescapable that all who are deemed fit for Baptism, no matter what their physical age, should also be confirmed within the same liturgical event. This seems to have in fact been the discipline in the Roman Church until the early Middle Ages, and it is still the practice of the Orthodox Churches."

"More"

Since Confirmation was so closely connected with Baptism, it is understandable that the word *more* is frequently used in the prayers. It is a matter of "more of the same" and also something special.

Besides being directed to the *activity* of Christians as witnesses, the prayers said during the celebration are concerned with *being* Christian. "Send your Holy Spirit to live in our hearts and make us temples of his glory." "Send the Holy Spirit to enlighten our minds." "Pour out the Holy Spirit upon them to strengthen them in their faith, and anoint them to be more like Christ." "Send your Holy Spirit to be their helper and guide." A special plea is made for the gifts of the Holy Spirit.

The "more" applies in other ways. As a result of the Christian community's public act of Confirmation, the baptized, according to Vatican II, "are endowed by the Holy Spirit with special strength. Hence they are more strictly obliged to spread and defend the faith both by word and deed as true witnesses of Christ" (Constitution on the Church, 11).

We are seeing the general and the special purpose of Confirmation. We are to follow Christ *more* closely and be more vigorously inspired by the Spirit received in Baptism, and we are also *more* strictly called to witness. Note that the ritual implies that witnessing is already our obligation from Baptism: "Reborn [in Baptism] as sons of God, *they must confess before men* the faith which they have received from God through the Church" (Constitution on the Church, 11).

Father Karl Rahner writes, "The Church has already given us the Word in Baptism. But she says it even *more* distinctly and *more* urgently in the word of grace of Confirmation. Our freedom is *again* awakened and gently invited to choose life."

Awareness

Since there is special reference to the Spirit of truth, Confirmation must be intended to influence our understanding and experience. We are made more fully aware of the dimensions of Christian life. Growing up includes understanding. I "see" much more clearly that my childhood self-centeredness is just that—a phase of life that is "childish" even though without guilt at the time. Now I see, or I begin to see.

Still we must be careful not to imply that Baptism implies a childish and self-centered stage of life, and Confirmation is a real beginning of Christian life, the "real" Baptism. Baptism includes awareness too; the emphasis in Confirmation is on the responsibility to take part in the Church's missionary life.

"Awareness" also connotes experience, that is, experiencing. Confirmation, like all sacraments, is a personal act of God and should somehow be a matter of psychological experience, not mere intellectual recognition.

The mystery of Christ is, first of all, an event and an experience, and only secondly a doctrine. So also is our Baptism and Confirmation and indeed all sacramental activity. Initiation should be an experience both for the individual and for the local Church.

Experiencing the love and mercy of God does not mean we are on a perpetual "high." The proof of love is faithfulness during the spiritual dark nights that seem to be as frequent as those of the calendar. But most of us are in absolutely no danger of becoming fanatics. A visitor from Jupiter would scarcely mistake our Sunday mornings for New Year's Eve parties.

Power

Christ said, in the victory of his resurrection, "All power is given to me in heaven and on earth: go *therefore* and proclaim the good news to all nations."

At resurrection Jesus was "established Son of God in power." Pentecost meant that the fullness of Christ's power is now let loose visibly on earth in apostolic Christians.

Now there are no longer any limits; now, as God-man, raised to the height of glory, made Lord of heaven and earth, he sent the full force of God's love —the Spirit—flowing over the whole world and into the hearts of men, pouring out the love of God offering eternal happiness.

This power of the Spirit is now in our hands, and we must use it for the saving of the world.

Fullness, Maturity

As *another* sacrament of initiation, besides Baptism and Eucharist, Confirmation has a note of *fullness*. It is the fullness of Pentecost. As inseparable from Baptism, it celebrates more explicitly and emphatically the Spirit's role and the richness of its possibilities. It is a reminder that we are to grow to the "full measure of the maturity of Christ" and that the Spirit of God is to penetrate our lives completely.

God is infinitely patient; he knows that our lives will move in slow and gradual growth. But God cannot water down his desire for our union with him in the likeness of Christ. I *can* resist him, of course; but faith leaves me no real choice but to let him make me into a "perfect" Christian.

Confirmation has been called the sacrament of maturity, but this has nothing to do with physical or psychological maturity. It is *not* an initiation into adulthood and it is *not* the acceptance of Baptism by one who now presumably knows what he or she is doing. Baptism certainly doesn't call for "childish" Christians and Confirmation for mature ones.

What then? Remember that Confirmation belongs with Baptism. It is one of three sacraments of initiation. Perhaps it is best to say that Confirmation insists that God is calling the baptized Christian to a *mature* life—better, a maturing life, since it is never complete.

There is a lifetime of never-ending conversion facing even the most fervent adult who receives the Sacrament of Baptism; and there is the same span of ongoing growth toward mature Christian responsibility in one who receives Confirmation.

The effects are not miraculous and ecstatic. The Spirit is able to work where divinely-created faith and hope and love bring about a breakthrough of the human being to the freedom of the sons and daughters of God, to an authentic life.

St. Thomas Aquinas sets up this proportion: Bap-

141

tism is to Confirmation as human birth is to human growth and maturing. But "spiritual adulthood" is not chronological for him. According to him, the grace of the Sacrament of Confirmation makes even an infant spiritually mature—not with any reference to age or awareness, but solely with reference to the limitless transforming power of grace which is available and which will be gradually experienced.

Wait Till 21

It is understandable that some would like to postpone Confirmation until a person is able to make a conscious and wholehearted commitment to Christ. But this is a question of Baptism, not Confirmation. As we saw in our discussion of infant Baptism, the parents and the Church promise to give the new Christian such love and example that he or she will gradually be drawn to full commitment to Christ. *No new sacrament is needed for this.* There may be a place and time for a renewal of Christian commitment (in fact, there is: the annual Easter Vigil Mass with its celebration of all three sacraments of initiation), but to say that Confirmation is the "real" Baptism is to ignore its purpose.

Actually, the logic of the Church's theology of initiation would seem to call for all three sacraments of initiation for infants! The ritual itself says that Confirmation is generally "postponed" until about the seventh year.

There is a possible Pelagian ("I can save my own soul") danger in the theory of "waiting until one is ready." There is a very Christian implication in infant Baptism (and Confirmation, or Confirmation at an

early age). It is simply this: Conversion, salvation, grace, holiness, etc., are God's gifts. They are not acquired in any way, shape or form by human effort. And there is no better symbol of this than their being given before any human effort to acquire them.

Ralph Keifer, writing in *Worship* (48:7, p. 394), says, "The difficulty with retaining the practice of Confirmation at a later age and interpreting it as a sacrament of commitment or maturity is that this does serious damage to the understanding of a sacrament as an action of God as well as an action of man. Man's commitment is not the measure of God's grace."

The Special Purpose: Witness

We have perhaps mistakenly saved the best wine, or the fundamental purpose, till last—though it has inevitably appeared in connection with the various distinctive elements of the sacrament. Now it can be said that the "more" is a stricter call to *witness*; our *awareness* is of a Spirit-filled responsibility to witness God's saving love to others, a concern for the Church and the world guided by the Spirit; we have the *power* of Christ's Spirit to witness to his saving death and resurrection; and it is *full* power, able to effect the absolute victory of Christ, and to bring us to *mature* responsibility ourselves.

Confirmation is the communication of the Spirit for a particular task and for a special challenge: it strengthens Christians to confess their faith before the world, to bear witness to Christ and to continue the work of bringing all persons to the Father.

"The grace of Confirmation," Karl Rahner

writes, "is the Church's grace for carrying out her *mission* to the world, and for announcing the world's transfiguration. This grace must make [God's] acceptance of the world, for the latter's transfiguration, visible *in* the world."

Every Christian, the same theologian says, has his or her own special charism for the Church and for the world, a special task of a social and indeed of a "political" kind. This is not a merely profane or "natural" task.

Defense of the Faith

For some good reasons, we don't think of the adjective "militant" as a helpful description of the Church today. But, as Father Christopher Kiesling, O.P., writes, "An attack on Christian values calls forth our awareness, injected in us by Confirmation, that the fullness of Christian life means unashamedly proclaiming Christ in such a situation. Our orientation toward Christian maturity, reinforced by Confirmation, inclines us actually to bear witness to Christ. If we do not succumb to fear but speak out, we are doing so because of our Confirmation, among other influences that may be at work."

Incidentally (or perhaps not!) the slap on the cheek, which was all that most kids remembered about Confirmation, was not, historically, a hint of the blows that were to come in defending the faith. It was rather the pat on the back that a father or mother gives their child as he or she goes forth to do a task.

Within the Whole Community

Our witness is carried out wherever we are—at

home, at work, at play; by word of mouth and by silence; but especially and above all by the testimony of daily life and action. For many people, this seems to be done in isolation: for instance, in what at least appears to be the pagan atmosphere of an office or a factory. But the Christian is not alone. He or she remembers (or should!) that it was within a community that the special commission to witness was given.

A confirmed Christian is one who has a permanent status (the "character" of Confirmation) in the *Church*. Christians are not ecclesial Lone Rangers without even a Tonto to comfort them. Their lives may indeed be without visible emotional support from the parish "community" to which they belong. So much the worse for that "community." But there is the strong comfort of faith that one is united to Christians all over the world and in history.

The Dying

Why does the Church call for the dying to receive this sacrament if they have not already done so? The answer would seem to be: so that they may be *fully* incorporated into the whole of Christ's redeeming activity and victory: his life, death, resurrection, glorification and establishment in power, and his sending of the Holy Spirit.

As we have said, the public mission of the Holy Spirit is part of the whole activity of Christ in saving us. The Church is fully the Church by the presence of the Spirit giving the members of Christ a share in the fullness of his power to save the world. Even in the moment of death—perhaps especially at the moment of death—the Christian witnesses with power to the saving presence of Christ's Spirit.

Actually, the law of the Church does require a person to receive the sacrament. Canon 787 states: "Although this sacrament is not necessary as a means of salvation, no one may, given the occasion, neglect to receive it." It is not considered a *serious* obligation —if we are pressed to answer that legal question.

A much more important question is, "How can we, fully brought into the Body of Christ by Baptism, Confirmation and Eucharist, become more Christ-like, more filled with his spirit, better witnesses of the love of God to each other and to all the world?" The first answer is (though other particular ones must follow), "Be sealed with the Gift of the Holy Spirit."

Appendix: "Baptism in the Spirit"

A great modern theologian, Father Karl Rahner, S.J., has written a little booklet entitled *A New Baptism in the Spirit: Confirmation Today* (Denville, New Jersey: Dimension Books, $1.95.)

He notes the longing for the experience of the Spirit and its power in today's world, and says there is no need to dispute the fact that "there can be especially striking and liberating experiences of grace, strengthening individuals to make radical transformations in their lives, giving to men and women (and making them feel for a long time) the stamp of Christian life and virtue. Taken all together these can be called (if you will) 'Baptism of the Spirit.' "

He hopes for a new and revitalized understanding of Confirmation, the Sacrament of the Spirit, the sacrament of mission and witness. He discusses the

147

problem as to whether or not the charismatic results of imposition of hands in Acts was (or should be today) a sacramental effect. He notes that, for Paul, even ordinary aptitudes in the service of the community are understood as charismatic gifts of the Spirit. He says, "We do not need to seek for a Baptism in the Spirit, understood as being a datum at a particular point in time, as a unique experience of rebirth, although it should not be denied that such an experience can occur in the life of some Christians."

For Rahner, these are instances in which we experience the Holy Spirit: "When a single sustaining hope enables us to face courageously both the enthusiastic highs and depressing lows of our daily earthly existence; when a responsibility freely accepted continues to be carried out, though it no longer bears any visible promise of success or usefulness; . . . when we no longer have any proof of the total value of life's actions, and yet have the strength to view them as positive in God's eyes; . . . when the bitter and disappointing and trying events of every day are endured serenely and patiently even to the last day; . . . when one dares to pray in silence and darkness and knows that he is heard; . . . when one has reached the point of entrusting all his certainty and all his doubts to the silent and encompassing mystery that he now loves above his personal achievements. . . ."

"When we hear the liberating promise of the Spirit in Church and experience his call, when we are 'Confirmed,' should we not let this unique word of promise be more and more alive in us for all the future of our life?"

The Rite of Confirmation
(Together With Baptism and Eucharist)

Baptism
Brief address to the newly baptized
Prayer
Imposition of hands
Anointing
Liturgy of Eucharist

The Rite of Confirmation (Apart from Baptism)

Liturgy of the Word
Presentation of the candidates
Homily
Renewal of baptismal promises
Imposition of Hands
Anointing: "Be sealed with the Gift of the Holy Spirit"
General intercessions
Liturgy of the Eucharist

Questions For Discussion

1. Is "giving good example" the same as "witness"?
2. What is the relation of Pentecost to Easter? Are there similarities between Confirmation and Baptism?
3. Do we receive the Holy Spirit in Baptism? What is the special purpose of Confirmation (besides the general purpose of all sacraments)?
4. Why is Confirmation not to be considered as a youthful or adult "real" Baptism? When do we "officially" renew our baptismal commitment?

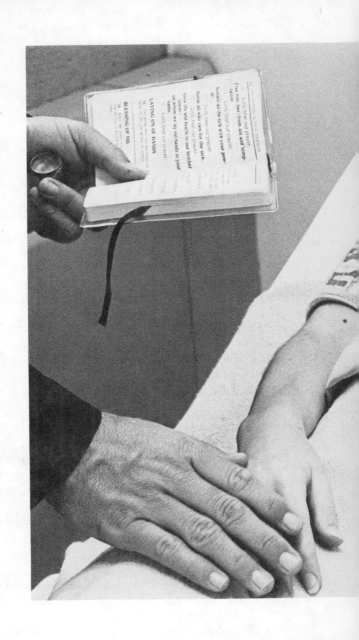

Chapter XV

Anointing of the Sick

Support in Suffering

there used to be a sweet old nun who was retired at one of the large hospitals conducted by her community. She regularly visited the patients, prayed and joked with them, and left everyone at least a bit more peaceful. After a while she became so arthritic that she had to give up her daily rounds, and was thereafter called for only in an emergency—when someone was dying. And that's where she got her name: "Sister Death." When *she* came, good heavens, it was all over. Make a will, forget the penicillin, kiss your friends goodbye. The Grim Reaper had sent an advance agent.

For too long a time the same thing has happened to what the Church now calls the Sacrament of the Anointing of the *Sick*. Spouses and relatives of the sick, hoping against hope, would wait until the poor man or woman was almost unconscious before calling the priest. They were afraid of scaring the sick person to death or, more likely, afraid to admit that their loved one was dying.

As a result, priests felt like "Father Death" when they were called to administer the sacrament. It was

extreme unction (kids naturally called it "extry munc-
tion" in school and for the rest of their lives)—the
last anointing.

Vatican II called for a return to an older understanding of the sacrament as one intended for those
who are seriously sick. They need not necessarily be
dying, except in the sense that any serious illness
poses some danger of death.

The new ritual is official but still provisional in
America. Issued by the Congregation for Divine
Worship on December 7, 1972, it says: " 'Extreme
Unction,' which may also and more fittingly be called
'Anointing of the Sick,' is not a sacrament for those
only who are at the point of death. Hence, as soon as
anyone of the faithful *begins* to be in danger of death
from sickness *or old age*, the appropriate time for him
to receive this sacrament has *certainly already arrived*
[emphasis added].

"A sick person should be anointed before surgery
whenever a dangerous illness is the reason for the surgery.

"Old people may be anointed if they are in weak
condition although no dangerous illness is present.

"Sick children may be anointed if they have sufficient use of reason to be comforted by the sacrament."

How long will it take us to forget the "Father
Death" image and welcome the priest for Anointing
with the same calmness we have when he brings Holy
Communion? The practice of group anointings of
older people in church is assuring *them*. But untradi-
tional traditions die hard.

It cannot be denied, of course, that sickness *is* a

signal we are going to die some day. Sickness-death are part of the wretched inheritance of mankind's sin. Sickness is a warning that we are mortal. But the Sacrament of the Sick is primarily interested in health—physical, emotional, spiritual, personal. The ritual is entitled: "The Rite of Anointing and Pastoral Care of the Sick." It *also* includes rites for the dying.

Other Elements in the New Ritual

The words said by the priest at the actual anointing are these: "Through this holy anointing may the Lord in his love and mercy help you with the grace of the Holy Spirit." (Response: "Amen.") "May the Lord who frees you from sin save you and raise you up." (Response: "Amen.") The person is anointed only on the forehead and on the hands. A single anointing is sufficient in emergency.

The celebration begins with the usual blessing, but a special point is made that the holy water recalls the person's baptismal sharing in Christ's redeeming passion and resurrection.

The words of St. James are part of the opening prayers: "Is there anyone sick among you? Let him call for the elders of the Church, and let them pray over him and anoint him in the name of the Lord. This prayer, made in faith, will save the sick man. The Lord will restore his health, and if he has committed any sins, they will be forgiven."

There is a penitential rite similar to that at the beginning of Mass, and a Scripture reading.

Formerly the priest "extended" his hand over the sick person. Now, the ritual says, he "lays his hands on the head of the sick person in silence." The laying on of hands was a familiar gesture in both Old and New Testaments and deserves more attention than we have usually given it. It is a moment of silent prayer that the Spirit of God come upon the person with healing power. It is (or should be) prominent in the rite of other sacraments (Baptism, Confirmation, Penance, Ordination) as a sign of the coming of God's power. In this sacrament it is also an expression of concern through the sense of touch.

The Lord's Prayer and Holy Communion are normally part of the celebration.

Another Sacrament of Faith

Perhaps more than any of the others, the Sacrament of Anointing runs the risk of magical or merely material expectations. Will the anointing remove the cancer from my mother's lungs? Will Aunt Mamie live 20 more years? The questions are crude, but they are important, human and understandable concerns. As they stand, they are merely medical questions asked of doctors, not the community of Christ.

Jesus was and is interested in people's bodily health. But he does not (supposing it is even possible) separate this from the total health of the person. The sacrament is for *sick* persons, but it is for sick *persons*.

Moreover, it is for sick persons who are disciples of Christ, those who have faith in him as the revelation of God's eternal saving love for us. To the degree that faith is present, the sacrament will be a holy and wholesome meeting with Christ. He will do what he wills, and the sick person will be at peace. To the degree that faith is not present, there is danger of a false interpretation of the sacrament.

The ritual says, "The anointing of the sick, which includes the prayer of faith (see James 5:15), is a sacrament of faith. This faith is important for the minister and particularly for the one who receives it. The sick man will be saved by his faith and the faith of the Church which looks back to the death and resurrection of Christ, the source of the sacrament's power, and looks ahead to the future kingdom which is pledged in the sacraments."

The sick person who is possessed by living faith is simply confident in the heart of Christ, which went out to those who were suffering in any way—to those whose eyes were without light as well as to those whose minds were dark, to those whose ears were deaf to their loved ones' voices as well as those who no longer heard the voice of God.

The Faith of the Church

Another consideration which must precede the consideration of particular questions is that of the presence of the Church community. Vatican II says: "By the sacred Anointing of the Sick and the prayer of her priests, the *whole Church* commends those who are ill to the suffering and glorified Lord, asking that he may lighten their suffering and save them. She exhorts them, moreover, to contribute to the welfare of the *whole people of God* by associating themselves freely with the passion and death of Christ" (Constitution on the Church, 11).

The Church, as we have said, is the Sacrament of Christ. Therefore the Church, as visibly as possible, should be present with the sick person when the sacrament is celebrated. As with other sacraments, the priest does indeed represent the whole Church; but the support and prayer of the Christian community is obviously more consoling when other persons are present. The ritual says: "The family and friends of the sick and those who take care of them have a special share in this ministry of comfort. It is their task to strengthen the sick with words of faith, and by praying with them, to commend them to the Lord who suffered and is glorified, and to urge the sick to unite themselves willingly with the passion and death of Christ for the good of God's people."

The new rite permits the anointing of several sick Christians in the same ceremony in a church or chapel. Group anointings may be celebrated during Mass after the Liturgy of the Word, or in a communion service, or in a distinct rite similar to the one introduced at Lourdes. Parishes may hold communal celebrations of the sacrament at regular intervals.

Clarifying the Purpose of the Sacrament

From the words of the rite and from other statements of the Church, we can now attempt to pinpoint the specific purpose of this sacrament.

Perhaps "pinpoint" is too strong a word. Our rational approach tends to put God's ever-embracing love into neat little pigeonholes, and we may come to think of his activity as stopping and starting, like a furnace that turns on and off according to the ups and downs of its thermostat.

God's gracious saving work never stops. All life is the means of grace. We do not think of the sacraments as supplying a "something" not otherwise given. They are, rather, the *visible* and *identifiable* and *unquestionable* moments of the ever-continuing "work" of Jesus and the Father and the Spirit.

The Sacrament of Anointing, then, is a particular moment in the long story of our salvation. In a particular and serious human situation—sickness—God assures the sick person, and all the rest of us, that his strength and love is more powerful than all evil, suffering, sin and death.

Suffering ennobles, they say; more often it angers and confuses. And sometimes it eats heart and hope out of a person.

"Sickness and pain," says the new ritual, "have always been a heavy burden for man and an enigma to his understanding. Christians suffer sickness and pain as do all other men; yet their faith helps them to understand better the mystery of suffering and to bear their pain more bravely. From Christ's words they know that sickness has meaning and value for their own salvation and for the world's. . . ."

The ritual then insists that sickness cannot be considered a punishment for one's personal sins, even though it is related to humanity's sinful condition. And since humanity *has* brought this sad condition upon itself, God wills that we struggle against it with all our resources.

Christians should be in the forefront of those fighting to wipe all disease from the face of the earth. At the same time they are called to "fill up what is lacking in the sufferings of Christ, for the salvation of the world." Suffering is not only conquered in the medical laboratory; Christ's grace must also destroy its destructive power in our hearts.

Why the Sacrament?

For one of the great problems of life, then, Christ has given an "answer." The Church uses words to remind the sick person of the broad picture of salvation: This sacrament too is concerned with life, love, grace, peace, salvation. The specific purposes of the Anointing of the Sick may be summed up as follows:

1) Strength against the particular temptations of sickness. When our bodies are healthy and vigorous and life flows smoothly, we have no reason to doubt the presence of a benevolent and entirely satisfying kind of Father; indeed, we may be content that he remains at a quite impersonal distance. But when we are helpless on our backs, and fear unsettles our judgment, we not only realize our radical helplessness but we are also *tempted to blame God for the fact that we are creatures*, and thus subject to the ultimate coming apart of the molecules of our body, and limited in the vision of our minds and the power of our will. Where was God, we wonder, when our body was broken in a car accident or our liver went bad from too much alcohol.

So Christ comes visibly and lays his hands on us and communicates power. It is a mother holding a baby that has awakened in terror; it is a friend holding a wounded friend in strong embrace. It is not that "answers" are given; rather it is a case of not really needing to put the questions.

In the words of the ritual, the one "who is seriously ill needs the special help of God's grace in this time of anxiety, lest he be broken in spirit and subject to temptations and the weakening of faith."

The powerful word of Christ is directed to helping the sick person reject the easy avenue of self-pity, impatience, discouragement, and even a lessening of faith and hope.

Within this basic purpose of the sacrament, others can be discerned:

2) The easing of suffering. The prayers of the Church use the word "ease" several times, along with "comfort," "lighten" and "relieve." The psychosomatic oneness of our person will always pose the question as to whether the relieving of our spirit is healing our body. We should avoid separating the "natural" and the "supernatural." They are distinct, but they exist together in God's plan for our eternal happiness. Why discount God's providential care if a calm mind and brave spirit improve my ailing blood pressure? Christ was and is interested in whole persons.

3) Trust and confidence in God. Inseparable from strength to reject the peculiar temptations of sickness and to accept God's "easing" is the grace to assert or reassert our confidence in God. We hope to be healed, and we turn to every reasonable "human" skill for this purpose. But we need a "heart for all seasons," a strength to live on when healing does not happen. Christ offers this confidence to those who will accept it. A cynical world calls such an attitude naive and superstitious—"pie in the sky." So be it. Trust has its own crosses to bear.

4) The forgiveness of sin. We recall that God is in the business of forgiving sin *all the time*. The peak moment of reconciliation *visibly* is the Sacrament of Penance. Therefore, the ritual says, "Whenever it is

159

necessary, the priest should hear the sacramental confession of the sick person, if possible, before the celebration of the Anointing." It also directs the priest that when death is near (presumably *not* the usual situation) and there is not enough time to administer the sacraments of Penance, Anointing and Eucharist, he should first give the sick person an opportunity for confession, then give Viaticum, and only then, if there is time, administer the Sacrament of Anointing.

The words accompanying the anointing, besides those quoted above, are: "May the Lord who frees you from sin save you and raise you up." This of course echoes the words of St. James, also quoted above: ". . . and if he has committed any sins, they will be forgiven."

The Council of Trent spoke of the sacrament as taking away sins, if any still remain to be taken away, "and the remnants of sin." What are these?

Sin is an attitude, and while we may be basically or even "totally" sorry, there can well be a residue of unwillingness that our "best" intention has not reached. Even supposing that our sinfulness has been removed to the last drop, the aftereffects of sin may remain — like the urge in a reformed drunkard.

Because we live in an age of nuts and bolts, the following terrible mechanical comparison may be forgiven. There are attitudes in us that resemble pieces of a machine that have been bent out of shape, more or less. Something is "sprung." The machine operates, but not as it really should. The bent and sprung pieces have to be restored to their proper shape before the machine will function with the efficiency the maker designed. So, the self-indulgence of sin has left us with attitudes that resemble the bent piece. Our basic attitude may be good, but beyond that, we have been damaged by our own history of sin. Our sinfulness may be forgiven; our faith in Christ may burn with such a fervor that even the traces of habit cannot assert themselves — but this is not the case with most of us. And the merciful Christ comes to heal this condition too.

The Healing of the Body

Let it be said again that God is interested in healing the *whole person*. Well, then, should not every cancer patient rise up with a sound body after celebrating this sacrament — or at least within a month or so?

There are those who say that we just don't have enough faith if this doesn't happen. Every time a sick person came to him in faith, they say, Jesus healed that person. He gave his apostles the gift of healing.

No doubt most of us don't have enough faith, or at least we could stand a lot of improvement. But it can hardly be said that all the persons who have not received complete bodily healing by this sacrament were without faith. Any of us could produce a list as evidence. And while the Gospels show Jesus' healings as *a sign that the power of God was irresistibly entering the world,* we need not suppose that every single friend of his whose body he embraced was healed or preserved from all sickness. Are we to believe that until Jesus' death his followers were all free from cancer, typhus, malnutrition, pneumonia, heart trouble, food poisoning and high blood pressure — not to speak of blindness, deafness, birth defects, etc.?

It sounds crude, put that way, but it seems the only way to counteract our sometimes crude questions. There is indeed a special gift of healing, apart from the sacrament, which God gives to those he pleases. But the sacraments *always* have their effect on those who celebrate them with faith. Since physical healing — at least complete healing, since there is always *some* physical effect—is not *always* the result of the sacrament, it must not be an essential purpose.

Still, we must be honest and not ignore the words of St. James about the Anointing of the Sick and the laying on of hands: "This prayer, made in faith, will save the sick man. The Lord will restore his health, and if he has committed any sins, they will be forgiven."

We are left with the traditional phrasing that goes back to the Council of Trent and which, perhaps, is the best way to talk about the mystery: The sick person will "sometimes regain bodily health, if this is expedient for the health of the soul."

There *is* an infallible physical result of Jesus' saving work, expressed through the sacraments: Our bodies will be, to say the least, "healed" forever by resurrection. Even death is a victory and a healing to the Christian.

Death

As we have said, the Sacrament of Anointing is not primarily concerned with death. The word "death" is not used in the rite except with reference to the death of Christ in two optional prayers.

But obviously the sacrament will also be given to those who are dying. The strength Christ gives for the trials of the sick is even more necessary for those who face imminent death. The same positive benefits that suffering can have, if accepted in faith, can be achieved by an enlightened attitude toward death.

Christ did not remove death; he beat death at its own game. He made death kill itself. In a sense, Christ's death was the "last" death; after that moment, death became the gate of heaven. Jesus expressed, in "commending his spirit" to the Father, the most perfect dependence a man could give to God. He said that *everything was from God,* most of all, life. In his death Jesus expressed the greatest possible self-giving love and trust of the Father. In the mystery of his divinity and humanity, the man who sweat blood in terror threw himself into the darkness of death in utter trust, knowing even as he cried in agony that his Father was faithful.

The Christian is thus enabled to see death as his final, wholehearted act of union with Christ and with the Father. He says, "My life is yours, O Father."

Summing Up

This sacrament, which must be seen as part of the larger work of God's saving love, is God's visible response to one of the major problems of life: sickness. Its purpose is to meet the particular temptations that come with sickness, and to promote the health of the whole person. It is Christ's assurance that all evil, suffering, sickness and death are destroyed by his victorious death and resurrection.

The Rite of Anointing of the Sick

Introductory Rites

Greeting and optional sprinkling with holy water
as a reminder of Baptism
Opening address or prayer
Confession or a penitential rite as at Mass

Liturgy of the Word

Scripture readings
The reading or readings to be used should be
selected from the 79 options given in the new ritual. They should be chosen to correspond to the
physical and spiritual condition of the sick person and read by the priest or one of those present.
Litany of intercession, which can include spontane-
ous petitions (may be postponed to follow the
actual anointing)

Liturgy of Anointing

Imposition of hands (in silence)
Thanksgiving over the oil (or blessing of oil)
Anointing on forehead and hands
"Through this holy anointing may the Lord in
his love and mercy help you with the grace of the
Holy Spirit." R. Amen.
"May the Lord who frees you from sin save you
and raise you up." R. Amen.
Prayer after anointing (adapted to the sick person's
condition)

Conclusion

The Lord's Prayer

Communion, as in the rite for communion of the
  sick (optional)
Blessing

Questions For Discussion

1. Since death is the result of mankind's sin, how
   does sickness in general fit into the picture?
2. How would you explain God's allowing suffering
   for the sake of freedom?
3. What steps would you take to change the notion
   that the Sacrament of the Sick is "a sign you're
   going to die"?
4. What hopes of healing would you have if you
   received this sacrament?
5. What is the significance of the community (family, relatives, friends) gathered around the sick
   person for the sacrament?

Chapter XVI

Penance

Reconciliation to God and Community

the last of the sacramental rites to be revised was that of confession, or, as the new emphasis indicates, the Sacrament of Reconciliation.

The new ritual will probably be disappointing to some Catholics. There is not that much difference in the actual ceremonies and words compared with the old form. In fact, if you want to be downright factual about it, all the penitent is really required to say in the new rite (besides the confession of sin) is: an Act of Contrition, the Sign of the Cross, Amen (twice) and a response — which may easily be forgotten — "His mercy endures forever."

Other Catholics — and maybe the disappointed ones — will sense that there is more here than a rephrasing of absolution. The Church thinks long thoughts, and the revision of the rites is part of what the Church's plan must always be: to help our whole lives be a never-ending conversion to Christ. It is the theology and spirit of the new ritual that must get our attention. It is not new, and yet some emphases are here which have been overshadowed in recent centuries. Some things, of course, remain the same: the mercy of God, the evil of sin, and the reconciling mission of the Church.

We'll continue with what we've tried to do throughout this book: insist on the principal facts about every sacrament:

1) God is warm and forgiving.
2) Sin is a deep pervasive fact in our lives.
3) The Church is Jesus' reconciling community.

A Warm, Forgiving God

Among the essentials of the sacrament, the most obvious should be: God is a warm, loving, forgiving God. The primary fact about the sacrament of confession is that God loves us so much that like "The Hound of Heaven" in Francis Thompson's famous poem he will never stop pursuing us so that he may heal our agony and our aloneness. If we do not have the fundamental realization that we are approaching a merciful God, a passionately loving God, then the sacrament can become merely an ordeal — something you go through, so that when you come out you have a ticket that says that God has nothing on you.

This is not the thrust of the ritual at all. The overwhelming truth about the Sacrament of Reconciliation is that God wants to heal us more than we want to be healed. But this God must be seen in his warmth, and therefore we always must come back to the glorious fact of the Incarnation of the Second Person of the Trinity. God wanted to speak to us in our language, to touch us with flesh like our own, to look into our eyes with human eyes and to speak to us with human words. And so we have Jesus, the sign that is the sacrament of the loving God.

If anyone wanted to know how good God was, all he needed to do was to look at Jesus, listen to him and receive his healing. It is the same today. We need to realize that this same divine and human Jesus is eagerly and ardently welcoming us to reconciliation and healing and peace. He is not interested in punishment and bawlings out. We must first experience his love, and it will prompt us to take care of whatever reparation and reform is needed.

Sin: The Rest of the Iceberg

One way of describing what is "happening" to sin these days is to say that the ocean is draining away and leaving the iceberg completely visible. Only the tip of the iceberg used to be visible — perhaps one-seventh of the whole. Now the whole thing is being examined — the foundations, the basis, the deep roots, the *reason* why something stuck out above the surface of the water.

There is much more to sin than meets the eye. We have always been well aware of that tip of the iceberg: all of the visible, countable things, from missing Mass to murder, from slander to adultery. These can be identified, counted, confessed.

But let's take a look at the rest of the iceberg. What's supporting this adultery? What are the roots of this murder? If you melt away the tip, is the whole iceberg gone? If you're sorry for the top, what do you do about the bottom?

Looking at the whole iceberg, we see not only individual thefts, sneers, slanders, lustings, broken laws — but attitudes constructed (frozen?) over a long period of time. Attitudes that lie beneath the surface of our lives all the time, just as six-sevenths of the iceberg floats invisible beneath the visible tip. These are attitudes that enable us, for instance, to *omit* countless words of concern, gestures of sympathy, actual responses to the needs we see in other people; attitudes of resentment, self-pity, selfishness, vindictiveness that lie hidden within even "pious" practices like going to Mass, "doing our duty," "saying" our prayers. These are attitudes of deliberate non-involvement with the problems of people around us, problems of society in general ("Well, what do you expect one individual like me to do?"). We have all discovered (easily in others, not so easily in ourselves) deep racist attitudes ("Of course I have nothing against them personally"), ultra-nationalism ("My country, right or wrong"), neglect ("We put mother into a licensed home, didn't we?"), plain injustice ("It's OK, I'm on an expense account").

The bottom of the iceberg is hard to put into categories. It's not pure ice; it's a *mixture* of pride, selfishness, self-centeredness, self-hatred, indifference, laziness, rebellion.

When we think of sin — and of forgiveness and a better life — we must therefore go beneath the surface of the external acts. Sin starts inside. It is a decision. It is many decisions. It is a growing habit, an attitude. The disease can have many external symptoms—and these are terribly important, no one is denying that—but we must seek the cause and the cure below the surface of our lives.

The death-producing act called mortal sin comes from the depths of the iceberg — the willingness to reject God's offer of life, love, holiness, happiness.

God is constantly calling to us, in every circumstance of our life, to respond to him, to come to him as he calls to us from other persons, to accept his love as it is given to us by other persons.

We can decide not to accept this relationship with God. It costs too much. We make arrangements to avoid it politely — omitting this, avoiding that, rationalizing this. An attitude grows.

If this attitude is allowed to grow far enough, it becomes a decision that fills our whole life. The adultery, the slander, the hatred, the broken friendship, the ignoring of need is a decision that comes out of a whole life-decision.

Sinfulness is not something that we turn on and off like an electric switch. What somebody does at 12:05 represents that attitude he had at noon and 11:30 and 11, and the attitude that he still has at 1 and 2 and 3 o'clock unless he makes a definite effort to change the spirit which is filling his life.

We Catholics have sometimes been puzzled that Protestants couldn't understand that stealing 50 cents was "only" a venial sin, whereas stealing a thousand dollars was obviously serious. They were saying, it seems, that if you steal one thing there is no reason to think that you will not steal anything else, no matter how valuable, and that sin should not be divided into "serious" and "venial." We might well adopt this attitude to the extent of saying that "stealing 50 cents is *not necessarily* a sign of a seriously sinful attitude as yet."

For sin, being an attitude, is a matter of degree. It is a refusal of God's love. Now, love can be rejected completely — divorce — or it can be rejected partially — relatively minor selfishness between husband and wife. So it is with our relationship with God. I can refuse God's call to love this person at this particular moment in this particular way, by a word said or not said, by a gesture, by doing nothing.

Now, taking this act *as if* it were isolated from the rest of my life (an impossible supposition), it is not serious. It does not break my relationship with God. But of itself it has no place to go except in that direction. Selfishness, greed, self-centeredness have no built-in governor on them; they grow by what they feed on.

And so nothing is "only" a venial sin, just as the first few cells affected by cancer are not "just a few little cancer cells." It *should* be very easy to stop the whole thing right there. Very often it is. But nobody in his right mind says, "This is just a cancer cell."

We are dealing with interior decisions and attitudes, freely accepted values. We are choosing in a basic or a relatively "minor" way to ignore and reject the personal approach of a loving God.

Sin Is Social

A great emphasis at least implicit in the new ritual is the socialness of sin. Evil gets hardened in the structures of society, of family life, of individual life. The world is blotched with the results of some people's sin, making or leaving other people ignorant, poor, deprived of elementary rights, starving physically, emotionally and intellectually. Marriage and family life can settle into routine coldness, breaks in communication, isolation — to the lifelong damage of both spouses and children.

Some sins are evidently social — striking someone in the face, taking his money, ruining his reputation, spreading disease of mind or body. But the deepest reason why sin is social lies in the very way God made us. We are meant to form a loving community, one in which members help (not hinder) each other to reach full development as human beings and as God's family.

Sorrow: The Prodigal Son "Comes To"

The best thing that can happen to one who freely enters the condition of mortal sinfulness is the realization of what he has lost. The greatest obstacle is the very nature of the sin itself: the gradually-induced blindness of mind and rigidity of heart that is part of the process of rejecting God.

But if the grace of the Father can be discovered again in the heart, real sorrow can follow. The Prodigal Son realizes, in the light of his father's love, that he has lost everything that was decent. It was his choice.

He is not suffering from cultural alienation, from being in a different country. His anguish is not that of one who is only emotionally upset. He is not an outcast—though that self-centered and merciless elder brother would have it so. His father did not disown him. He walked out freely.

So he admits the truth. He *is not worthy* to be his father's son. It is his own fault that he lies in misery. He has rejected love.

Now he rejects that rejection. He turns back from his senseless, selfish, childish, prideful ignoring of his father's love. He turns *away*, he turns *to*. He withdraws his choice of evil. He turns with all his heart to his father.

He is sorry for himself, of course, but mainly for his father. Not a pitying sorrow—as if his father had naively made demands no one could fulfill—but sorry that one so good, so trusting, should be betrayed by his own child. He sees all that sin is—the loss of all that is decent, the spoiling of a relationship, the rejection of a great love, the doom of emptiness.

The Church, the Reconciling Community

How do we see with our own eyes and hear with our own ears the human-divine warmth of Jesus' forgiveness? We see and hear and touch him in that group of people whom he has left behind to be precisely his visible presence, that group of people whom we call the Church. The Church is called to be the convincing sign of God's healing. To the degree that the Church—and that means the local parish—is a welcoming, forgiving, open, reconciling, Christlike community, they—we—are continuing the work of Christ on earth today.

The greatest help to reconciliation should be the inviting community. The sinner should not be left to sweat it out by himself, to finally decide to make an individual return to God after a long, lonely, harrowing experience of guilt and misery. We do not save ourselves. We are *drawn* to the Father by Christ, and to Christ by his people.

There is a second reason why the Church is involved in reconciliation. The Church is the sign and the reality of the persons I have hurt. My sinfulness sometimes inflicts harm on others directly—unkind words, revenge, injustice; sometimes indirectly—by all the things I do *not* do for others (the word of reconciliation, encouragement, acceptance).

For most people, this is a fairly airy argument. They still say, "But how does my sin hurt other people? How do I wound the Church by my sin? I can see that I am guilty myself. But I don't see what my personal sin has to do with anyone else except those whom I hurt directly, or those with whom I sin."

Let's think first of mortal sinfulness, a basic turning away from God at the core of my life, a real breaking of the relationship. Now, if anyone is capable of the greatest evil, if his attitude *is* and *remains* a willingness to deny God his rights and to refuse a relationship, such a person certainly is not going to feel any real responsibility toward any human being. Remember, we are not speaking of basically good people who rebel against a distorted idea of God, nor about those who may have sinned in the past but have rejected what they recognize to be evil. We are speaking of someone who knowingly and willingly accepts evil and rejects God in a basic way. With such an attitude, he or she is simply not capable of loving anyone.

The first evil such a one is doing to his neighbor is a refusal to love. Whatever the external show, he simply does not have the power or the intention to give goodness to anyone. He is a dead member of a living body. The other members may not even know what they are being denied.

This can be seen in what some have called the sinful state of society. We can be born into a culture that no longer even questions some evils: slavery, oppression, inequalities, racism, materialism, depersonalization.

Secondly, and obviously, we hurt each other by the external expression of our sinful attitude, by all the things we do not say, and by the hurtful things we say and do.

This spreading infection of our own sin hurts others on the level of venial sinfulness too. "Minor" though it is, our selfishness and self-seeking creates problems for others. Perhaps they have become so used to it that they no longer think about the pain we add to their lives, making them adapt to our whims and oddities, our stubbornness. Perhaps they have long since given up on receiving encouragement, understanding, sympathy or support from us.

Communal Aspect of Penance

Hence the sacrament of confession has always been a *reconciliation.* In the early Church, "public" sinners, those whose sins were publicly known, had to belong to a separate group of penitents. During their period of penance they could partake only in a minimal way in the Eucharistic sacrifice and meal. When the time of their penance was over, a dramatic ceremony took place. On Holy Thursday the bishop and the congregation would go to the front door of the church and welcome back to the Eucharist those who had been public sinners. This is the perfect sign of the Sacrament of Reconciliation. Over the centuries we have lost sight of this "publicness" to a degree.

Today there is an increased awareness that the Sacrament of Reconciliation should at least sometimes be celebrated communally, that is, by a public service in which a group of people, especially those who know each other, publicly expresses in prayer their desire to forgive and be forgiven the sins whereby they rejected the loving relationship with the Father and hurt each other. The Saturday afternoon lines outside the confessional were in a sense "communal" celebrations; everyone was admitting his sinfulness just by being there. But it is more expressive of the meaning of sinfulness and forgiveness if common prayers, general admission of sinfulness, common expression of sorrow and purpose of amendment, Scripture readings, etc. accompany the private confession of sins.

The Welcoming Priest

The priest stands at the center of the reconciling community. It is he who personally welcomes the sinner, speaks to him or her kindly, and speaks the words of Christ's forgiveness. If the community is not Christlike in its work of reconciliation, he at least must convince sinners that God loves them. If, on the other hand, the community is warm and receptive but the priest is rigid, legalistic, punitive or simply oblivious to the awesome task Christ has given him, the community and the sinner both suffer.

Christ Visibly Comes to Us

The sacrament, let us insist again, is the visibility of Christ's actions. We are not just wishing or wistfully hoping, or presuming, or wondering if God forgives us. *We have a visible assurance that the Christ who is always present with us,* whether we are alive or dead, *does forgive us.* It is a tangible proof of reconciliation to God and to the Church.

Again let us insist that it is *visibility* that we need. We are indeed forgiven by Christ as soon as we turn to him again. He wants our reconciliation with the Father to be as visible as the Prodigal Son's father coming down the road to meet his son.

It would hardly have been satisfactory if the Prodigal Son had merely *presumed* his father's forgiveness. No, we are flesh and blood. We need words and gestures and personal presence. It is not enough, as this book has attempted to say, that a child "knows" that his mother loves him. If she doesn't put her arm around him sometimes, he will never be really sure of her love.

So Christ, carrying on his acceptance of our flesh-and-blood life, makes himself visible in the sacramental act of the priest and penitent.

The best answer to the question "Why should I go to confession?" is "Because it is Christ's own way of making visible his Father's forgiveness. You need it. He wants to give it."

Celebration and Worship

Since the acts of Christ are joyful ones, victorious ones, totally devoted to the honoring of his Father, his acts in the sacrament of Penance must be the same. Since it is a moment of joy and restoration of friendship, it is a celebration. Since the whole Church is involved, the sacrament is a common celebration.

The Father is welcoming his son back to his family table. No lectures, no punishment, no new rules, no reluctant and martyr-like acceptance. The Father says, "Let us celebrate! This is a joyful day. My son who was lost has been found. The son who was dead is alive again."

Three Modes of Celebrating the Sacrament

There are three possible ways of celebrating the sacrament according to the new ritual. The first is technically called "the reconciliation of individual penitents"—that is, there is one priest and one penitent in a private confession, the kind we are familiar with. The second is communal celebration of the sacrament with individual private confession and absolution, a form already followed in some parishes. The third is general confession and general absolution in emergency cases.

Let's take the third first, since "general absolution" makes people perk up their ears like a fox getting wind of a chicken farm.

The new ritual says that "individual, integral confession and absolution remain the only ordinary way for the faithful to reconcile themselves to God and the Church, unless physical or moral necessity excuses." The ritual then describes this necessity as "grave need, namely when, in view of the number of penitents, sufficient confessors are not available to hear individual confessions properly within a suitable period of time, so that the penitents would, through no fault of their own, have to go without sacramental grace or Holy Communion for a long time."

The second mode of celebrating the sacrament is what many Catholics have already experienced: the communal celebration of the sacrament, with individual private confession and absolution.

We concentrate, then, on the first mode of celebrating, namely, the reconciliation of individual penitents.

First it should be said that there is an option of using the traditional confessional or coming face-to-face with the priest. The ritual asks the priest and penitent to prepare by prayer. Right here we have the key to a fruitful celebration of the sacrament. Imagine the difference it will make if the priest and the penitent, kneeling together in church, perhaps aloud, but at least silently, pray for light, for strength, for healing. The whole atmosphere of the sacrament is then charged with the presence of God.

Next comes the reading of the Word of God. This is one of the emphases of the new ritual. Some selection of the Bible chosen by the penitent or the priest is now read (or it may be read as part of the preparation for the sacrament). Now again, if we realize that the Bible is the living, personal, here-and-now voice of God calling us to conversion and to his grace, this can be a very dramatic and powerful help to contrition and conversion. The reading of the Word of God again permits of almost limitless alternatives. The priest or penitent may recite a portion of Scripture from memory or read it.

Then the penitent confesses his or her sins in whatever way seems best. There is nothing new here.

The priest is then called upon to help the penitent make a complete confession (if necessary), encourage him or her to true sorrow, give suitable counsel, instruct the penitent (if necessary), etc. The priest then imposes a penance, which "may suitably take the form of prayer, self-denial, and especially service of one's neighbor and works of mercy." These will underscore the social aspect of sin and its forgiveness.

Next the penitent expresses his or her sorrow for sin. This may be done in the traditional Act of Contrition or in the penitent's own words.

The priest imparts absolution while extending his hand(s) over the penitent. The new formula stresses that reconciliation comes from the Father, shows the connection between the reconciliation of the sinner and the death and resurrection of Christ, and stresses the role of the Holy Spirit in forgiveness. It also underlines the fact that reconciliation with God is asked for and given through the ministry of the Church. The penitent answers, "Amen."

The sacrament concludes quickly with a "proclamation of praise" of the mercy of God. The priest says "Give thanks to the Lord, for he is good," and the penitent responds, "His mercy endures forever." The priest then dismisses the penitent in these or similar words: "The Lord has freed you from your sins. Go in peace."

Using the new ritual means more than memorizing a few new phrases. We are being called to a deepening of our whole Christian life, particularly to a genuine repentance, a sense of the reconciling Christian community, and the ongoing, lifelong process of conversion. Above all, we are called to believe that we really have something to *celebrate*—namely, a visible sign of the reconciliation only God can give and which he generously offers.

The Rite of Reconciliation of One Penitent

Welcome by priest

Prayer
Reading of the Word of God
Confession
Expression of sorrow
Absolution
Proclamation of praise of God
Dismissal

The Rite of Reconciliation of Several Penitents
(Communal Celebration)

Song
Reading of the Word of God
Examination of conscience
Prayers
Confession and absolution (individual and private)
Proclamation of praise of God
Prayer
Dismissal

Questions For Discussion

1. Can we be personally reconciled to God any-where, anytime? How?
2. What is the basic reason why God uses the community of Christ as the visible sign of reconciliation?
3. If the Church, with priest as representative, is to be able to reconcile, what must be its "image" and spirit?
4. Discuss sin as an act and as an attitude.
5. What must precede reconciliation with God?
6. Do you think there is such a thing as a private sinfulness that affects no one else but yourself?

Conclusion

to put this book into a few words: The Father loved us so much he gave us his Son, visible in our human nature, even our mortal and wounded human nature. Christ is the Sacrament of God. Because he lived our life, our everyday actions can also be signs of God's own life. He went down into the depth of our misery, freely entering death. For his love and obedience, he was raised to glory; he is Lord of heaven and earth.

This Risen Christ, his human nature mysteriously transfigured, can meet us in his Spirit wherever matter embodies spirit, wherever spirit is incarnate. Through the visible community of brothers and sisters, his Body, he visibly continues the work of bringing all men together in the unity of his love.

In the Eucharist, he makes visible the love that already binds us together in him, nourishes and strengthens us with himself, accepts our love, goes with us in confidence to the Father.

We are enabled to share his dying and rising in Baptism, whereby he brings us to a new birth. In

Confirmation, he sends us to be himself visibly proclaiming the Good News in the power of his Spirit.

By priesthood, he gives us a visible center whereby to gather around him. The sign of his love in marriage makes all human life a sacrament of his presence. Lest the trial of sickness endanger our relationship with him, he comes to make it a means of deeper union.

And even when we have betrayed his love, totally or in part, he comes visibly to embrace us in reconciliation.

The Word was made flesh, and dwells among us. And we have seen his glory.